The Governance Regime of the Mekong River Basin

The Governance Regime of the Mekong River Basin

Can the Global Water Conventions Strengthen the 1995 Mekong Agreement?

By

Rémy Kinna and Alistair Rieu-Clarke

BRILL

LEIDEN | BOSTON

Library of Congress Control Number: 2017936794

Typeface for the Latin, Greek, and Cyrillic scripts: "Brill". See and download: brill.com/brill-typeface.

ISBN 978-90-04-34569-0 (paperback)
ISBN 978-90-04-34570-6 (e-book)

Originally published as Volume 2(1) 2017, in *International Water Law*, DOI 10.1163/23529369-12340005.

This book is printed on acid-free paper and produced in a sustainable manner.

Contents

Acknowledgments

A large part of the research for this academic monograph was based on a policy paper funded under the IUCN BRIDGE 'Building River Dialogue and Governance' project through the generous support of the Swiss Agency for Development and Cooperation. That IUCN policy paper was published in March 2016, and can be found here: http://www.3sbasin.org/publication/download-documents.html

The authors would also like to acknowledge the support provided by the University of Northumbria in order to make this publication open access.

Finally, Mr. Kinna would like to acknowledge the constant support and encouragement of Cristina Morgante.

The Governance Regime of the Mekong River Basin

Can the Global Water Conventions Strengthen the 1995 Mekong Agreement?

Rémy Kinna
Institute of Marine and Environmental Law, Faculty of Law,
University of Cape Town, South Africa
remy@transboundarywaterlaw.com

Alistair Rieu-Clarke
School of Law, Northumbria University, Newcastle, United Kingdom
alistair.rieu-clarke@northumbria.ac.uk

Abstract

Entry into force of the UN Watercourses Convention in August 2014, and the opening of the UNECE Water Convention to all states in March 2016, are significant milestones in international water law. A comparative analysis of these two global water conventions and the 1995 Mekong Agreement shows that all three instruments are generally compatible. Nonetheless, the international legal principles and processes set forth in the two conventions can render the Mekong Agreement more up to date, robust and practical. Strengthening the Agreement would be timely, given the increasing pressures associated with the rapid hydropower development within the basin and the gradually emerging disputes therein. Because of these fast-moving developments, the monograph strongly recommends that the Mekong states seriously consider joining both conventions in order to buttress and clarify key provisions of the 1995 Mekong Agreement.

Keywords

cooperation – dispute settlement – Mekong Agreement – sustainable development – UNECE Water Convention – UN Watercourses Convention

 | DOI 10.1163/9789004345706

Introduction

The Mekong River and its many tributaries flow through six countries (China, Myanmar, Laos, Thailand, Cambodia and Vietnam). Seventy million people are reliant upon the river to sustain their livelihoods.[1] In order to foster cooperation between the states of the Mekong Basin, the Agreement on the Cooperation for the Sustainable Development of the Mekong River Basin (Mekong Agreement) was adopted in 1995.[2] At the time of its adoption, the Mekong Agreement was heralded as epitomizing a flexible agreement that could effectively govern the Mekong River Basin in an equitable and sustainable manner.[3] This aspiration was reinforced by the establishment of the Mekong River Commission (MRC), which, as envisaged within the Mekong Agreement, offered an intergovernmental platform to further develop cooperation amongst the states of the Mekong River Basin.[4] Twenty years on from its adoption, the ability of the Mekong Agreement and the MRC to make effective and collective decisions pertaining to major infrastructure developments within the basin, and hydropower in particular, has been called into question.[5]

Entry into force of the United Nations Convention on the Law of the Non-navigational Uses of International Watercourses (UN Watercourses Convention)[6] in August 2014 constituted a fundamental milestone in the development of the

1 S. Pech & K. Sunada, '*Population Growth and Natural-Resources Pressures in the Mekong River Basin*', 37:3, AMBIO (2008) 219–224.

2 Agreement on the Cooperation for the Sustainable Development of the Mekong River Basin (1995).

3 G.E Radosevic & D.C. Olson, 'Existing and Emerging Basin Arrangements in Asia: Mekong River Commission Case Study', paper presented at World Bank, Third Workshop on River Basin Institution Development, 24 June 1999, Washington, D.C.

4 Chapter IV, Mekong Agreement.

5 E.B. Backer, 'The Mekong River Commission: Does It Work, and How Does the Mekong Basin's Geography Influence Its Effectiveness?' 26(4) Journal of Current Southeast Asian Affairs (2007) 32–56; R.K. Paisley, P. Weiler & T. Henshaw 'Trans-boundary Waters Governance Through The Prism of the Mekong River Basin', in J. Gray, C. Holley & R. Rayfuse, (eds), *Trans-jurisdictional Water Law and Governance* (London: Routledge 2016) 43–61; C. Sneddon and C. Fox 'Rethinking Transboundary Waters: Critical Hydropolitics of the Mekong Basin', 25 Political Geography (2006) 181–202; P. Hirsch, et al., *National Interests and Trans-boundary Water Governance in the Mekong* (Sydney: Mekong Resource Centre 2006); O. Hensengerth, 'Trans-boundary River Cooperation and the Regional Public Good: The Case of the Mekong River', 31 Contemporary Southeast Asia: A Journal of International Strategic Affairs (2009), 326–49; B. Bearden, 'The Legal Regime of the Mekong River: A Look Back and Some Proposals for the Way Ahead', 12 Water Policy (2010) 798–821.

6 Convention on the Law of the Non-navigational Uses of International Watercourses (1997), UN Doc. A/Res/51/229.

law relating to international watercourses.[7] The significance of entry into force of the UN Watercourses Convention was heightened in the Mekong region due to the fact that it was Vietnam, a party to the Mekong Agreement, that was the 35th country to become a party to the UN Watercourses Convention. As the 35th party to join the UN Watercourses Convention, Vietnam triggered the Convention's entry into force.[8] The UN Watercourses Convention, adopted in 1997, is considered to be, in most parts, a reflection of customary international law.[9] As a global framework convention, the UN Watercourses Convention's primary function is to provide a flexible legal framework in which watercourse-specific agreements can be developed, interpreted and implemented.

In parallel to the progressive number of states joining the UN Watercourses Convention, the UN Economic Commission for Europe's Convention on the Protection and Use of Transboundary Watercourses and International Lakes (UNECE Water Convention)[10] which was adopted under the auspices of the UNECE—a pan-European inter-governmental economic institution—underwent a process of amendment in order to allow states outside the UNECE region to become party to it. The decision to amend the UNECE Water Convention was made in November 2003 at the Third Meeting of the Parties, held in Madrid, Spain,[11] and the amendment eventually came into effect in March 2016.[12] Now any state can join the UNECE Water Convention, including states of the Mekong River Basin.

In light of calls to reform and strengthen the Mekong governance regime, it is pertinent to consider what the two conventions now operating at the global level, either individually or collectively, might offer. Can the similarities and differences between the two global water conventions be capitalised upon in order to help strengthen the existing Mekong Agreement in order to provide

7 'UN Watercourses Convention Enters into Force', http://www.unwaercoursesconvention.org/news/united-nations-watercourses-convention-enters-into-force (accessed 23 November 2016).

8 Article 36 of the UN Watercourses Convention provides that, '[t]he present Convention shall enter into force on the ninetieth day following the date of deposit of the thirty-fifth instrument of ratification, acceptance, approval or accession with the Secretary-General of the United Nations.'

9 S. McCaffrey, 'The Contribution of the UN Convention on the Law of the Non-navigational Uses of International Watercourses' 1(3/4) International Journal of Global Environmental Issues (2001) 250–263.

10 Convention on the Protection and Use of Transboundary Watercourses and International Lakes (1992).

11 UNECE, Amendment to articles 25 and 26 of the Convention, 12 January 2004, UN Doc. ECE/MP.WAT/14.

12 UNECE, https://www.unece.org/env/water.html (accessed 5 December 2016).

a more complete legal framework for the Mekong River Basin? This monograph seeks to tackle this timely question. In so doing, the monograph begins by outlining the global legal architecture for transboundary watercourses and discussing the global significance of the UN Watercourses Convention's entry into force and the opening up of the UNECE Water Convention. An overview of the objective and normative content of both conventions is then offered, before a detailed investigation of the compatibility of the three instruments. Finally, recommendations are made for strengthening the governance of the legal regime of the Mekong River Basin. These recommendations indicate that the benefit of Mekong riparian states joining both the UN Watercourses Convention and the UNECE Water Convention would be considerable for the people who live in the region and rely on its resources.

A Evolution, Overview and Status of the UN Watercourses Convention, the UNECE Water Convention and the Mekong Agreement

I *The UN Watercourses Convention*

(a) Evolution and Status

Agreements governing international watercourses can be traced back as far as 2,500 BC, yet this field of law largely gathered pace in the second half of the 20th century.[13] Much work needs to be done to strengthen arrangements pertaining to the world's international watercourses. Watercourse agreements are generally bilateral in nature and are largely developed, signed and ratified by those countries whose borders are adjacent to, or encompass, the international watercourse in question.[14] Only approximately 40 percent of the world's 263 international watercourses are now covered by a basin-specific agreement, which suggests that a significant number of basins are reliant upon customary international law.[15] The need to strengthen governance arrangements pertaining to transboundary waters has been recognised by some UN agencies with a mandate related to water. They observed that:

13 S.C. McCaffrey, 'The Evolution of the Law of International Watercourses', 5(2) Austrian Journal of Public and International Law (1996) 87–111.

14 N. Zawahri & S. McLaughlin, 'Fragmented Governance in International Rivers: Negotiating Bilateral Versus Multilateral Treaties', 44 International Studies Quarterly (2011) 835–858.

15 UN-Water, 'Transboundary Waters: Sharing Benefits, Sharing Responsibilities', UN-Water Thematic Paper, 2008, http://www.unwater.org/downloads/UNW_TRANSBOUNDARY.pdf (accessed 24 November 2016), at 6.

> ... existing agreements are sometimes not sufficiently effective to promote integrated water resources management due to problems at the national and local levels such as inadequate water management structures and weak capacity in countries to implement the agreements as well as shortcomings in the agreements themselves (for example, inadequate integration of aspects such as the environment, the lack of enforcement mechanisms, limited—sectoral—scope and non-inclusion of important riparian states).[16]

The need to strengthen governance arrangements pertaining to the world's international watercourses was already highlighted by the UN in the latter half of the 20th century. The UN began exploring legal problems relating to international watercourses following adoption of a UN General Assembly Resolution in 1959.[17] This initial resolution, which called for the UN Secretary General to take up a study of the legal problems relating to international rivers, was duly carried out and completed in 1963.[18] A supplementary report was produced by the UN Secretary-General in 1974.[19] Both reports surveyed existing state practice relating to international rivers as a precursor by which general rules and principles on the subject could be formulated. Based on the preliminary report by the UN Secretary-General, the UN General Assembly took the decision to recommend that the International Law Commission (ILC) take up the study of the law of the non-navigational uses of international watercourses, 'with a view to its progressive development and codification.'[20]

The ILC worked on the topic of the law of the non-navigational uses of international watercourses from 1971 to 1994.[21] This work involved an extensive

---

16 Ibid., at 6. See also, UNEP, GEF & UNEP-DHI Centre on Water and Environment, *Transboundary River Basins—Status and Trends* (Nairobi: UNEP, 2016), at 110.

17 UN General Assembly Resolution 1401(XIV), Preliminary Studies on the Legal Problems Relating to the Utilisation and Use of International Rivers, 21 November 1959, UN Doc. A/RES/1401(XIV).

18 UN Secretary-General, Legal Problems Relating to the Utilisation of International Rivers', UN Doc. A/5409.

19 UN Secretary-General, Legal Problems Relating to the Non-navigational Uses of International Watercourses—Supplementary Report by the Secretary-General, 25 March 1974, UN Doc. A/CN.4/274.

20 UN General Assembly Resolution 2669 (XXV), Progressive Development and Codification of the Rules of International Law Relating to International Watercourses, 8 December 1970, UN Doc. A/RES/2669(XXV).

21 S.C. McCaffrey, 'An Assessment of the Work of the International Law Commission', 36 Natural Resources Journal (1996) 297–318.

exercise in surveying state practice and consulting with states through the UN General Assembly, as well as surveys and questionnaires, in order to develop a set of draft articles that would be acceptable to all states.[22] The task was formidable: to reach a globally agreed-upon set of baseline legal principles and processes for governing transboundary rivers between two or more states. Key areas of disagreements, particularly between upstream and downstream states, related to: the definition of an international watercourse; the treatment of existing agreements; the relationship between equitable and reasonable utilisation, and no significant harm; the extent of the obligation to notify of planned measures; and the compulsory nature of dispute settlement mechanism.[23] The complexity of negotiations and difficulties in reaching consensus on these matters explains the length of time the ILC took to adopt a final set of draft articles. However, a testament to the quality of the ILC's work on the topic was reflected in the decision that the General Assembly took in 1994 to use the draft articles as a basis by which to, 'elaborate a framework convention on the law of the non-navigational uses of international watercourse.'[24]

The negotiation of the UN Watercourses Convention took place within the sixth committee of the UN General Assembly from 7 to 25 October 1996 and 24 March to 4 April 1997. The areas where it proved difficult to research consensus during the work of the ILC resurfaced during the negotiations within the sixth committee of the UN General Assembly.[25] However, states were able to reach a conclusion of the work on 21 May 1997, when the UN

22 See for example, ILC, Replies of Governments to the Commission's Questionnaire, 1 April 1976, UN Doc. A/CN.4/294 & Add. 1; ILC, Replies of Governments to the Commission's Questionnaire, 13 July 1979, UN. Doc. A/CN.4/324; ILC, Replies of Governments to the Commission's Questionnaire, 10 March & 3 July 1980, UN Doc. A/CN.4/329 & Add.1; ILC, Replies of Governments to the Commission's Questionnaire, 18 February & 28 June 1982, UN Doc. A/CN.4/352 & Add. 1; ILC, Comments and Observations Received from Governments, 3 March, 15 April, 18 May and 14 June 1993, UN Doc. A/CN.4/447 & Add. 1–3.

23 See E. Schroeder-Wildberg, 'The 1997 International Watercourses Convention—Background and Negotiations', Working Paper on Management in Environmental Planning, 2002, https://www.landschaftsoekonomie.tu-berlin.de/fileadmin/a0731/uploads/publikationen/workingpapers/wp00402.pdf (accessed 24 November 2016).

24 UN General Assembly Resolution 49/52, Draft Articles on the Law of the Non-Navigational Uses of International Watercourses, 9 December 1994, UN Doc. A/Res/49/52.

25 See A. Rieu-Clarke, 'Determining Sovereign Rights and Duties over International Watercourses: The Contribution of the International Law Commission and the UN General Assembly', in T. Tvedt, O. McIntyre & T.K. Woldetsadik, (eds), *A History of Water—Sovereignty and International Water Law* (London: I.B. Tauris 2015) 149–174.

Watercourses Convention was adopted.[26] At the time of its adoption, the UN Watercourses Convention was sponsored by 28 states, including Cambodia, Lao People's Democratic Republic and Vietnam.[27] A vote was also taken on the adoption of the convention, with 103 states voting in favour (including Cambodia, Lao People's Democratic Republic, Thailand and Vietnam), three states voting against (including China) and 26 states abstaining.[28]

Given this overwhelming support for the UN Watercourses Convention within the UN General Assembly, it might be questioned why it took until 2014 for the instrument to enter into force. Several reasons have been put forward for this lengthy period. Salman points to a number of contentious issues and misunderstandings concerning the content of the UN Watercourses Convention.[29] Other suggested reasons include treaty congestion, lack of awareness of the Convention and capacity to consider the benefits of ratification within government departments, and a lack of champions promoting the Convention.[30] In 2006, the Worldwide Fund for Nature (WWF) and its partners embarked on a concerted effort to address the reasons that were slowing down ratification of the Convention.[31] Through a suite of training and awareness-raising activities, this resulted in the Convention's entry into force in 2014. Activities to further promote the Convention have continued since its entry into force.[32] These activities include a meeting of parties to the UN Watercourses Convention, regional and international organisations and others, which took place at UN Education, Scientific and Cultural Organisation (UNESCO) headquarters in Paris on 15 and 16 September 2016.[33]

---

26 UN General Assembly Resolution 51/229, Convention on the Law of the Non-Navigational Uses of International Watercourses, 8 July 1997, UN Doc. A/Res/51/229.

27 UN General Assembly Official Records, 51st Session, 99th Plenary Meeting, 21 May 1997, UN Doc. A/51/PV.99.

28 Ibid.

29 S.M.A. Salman, 'The United Nations Watercourses Convention Ten Years Later: Why Has its Entry into Force Proven Difficult?', 32 *Water International* (2007) 1–15.

30 A. Rieu-Clarke & F.R. Loures, 'Still Not in Force: Should States Support the 1997 UN Watercourses Convention? 18(2) Review of European, Comparative & International Environmental Law (2009) 185–197.

31 See WWF, Water Conventions, http://wwf.panda.org/what_we_do/how_we_work/policy/conventions/water_conventions (accessed 24 November 2016).

32 See activities listed infra note 111.

33 UNESCO, 'Historic Gathering of the Parties to the 1997 UN Watercourses Convention at UNESCO', 15 September 2015, http://en.unesco.org/news/historic-gathering-parties-1997-watercourses-convention-unesco (accessed 24 November 2016).

(b) Overview

The overarching objective of the UN Watercourses Convention is to, 'ensure the utilisation, development, conservation, management and protection of international watercourses and the promotion of the optimal and sustainable utilisation thereof for present and future generations.'[34] While the need for a global framework instrument was recognised by states,[35] there was considerable debate over the appropriate scope of the Convention.[36] Ultimately, a compromise was sought whereby the Convention applies to the, 'uses of international watercourses and of their waters for purposes other than navigation and to measures of protection, preservation and management related to the uses of those watercourses and their waters.'[37] The use of the term 'watercourse' was preferred over the term 'drainage basin',[38] given that some states were concerned that the latter term would, 'leave open the possibility of undue and unacceptable restrictions which would affect not only the watercourse in question but also all those which constitute it, as well as those in the geographical areas through which they pass.'[39] The term 'watercourse' is defined in the Convention as meaning, 'a system of surface waters and groundwaters constituting by virtue of their physical relationship a unitary whole and commonly flowing into a common terminus';[40] and an 'international watercourse' as meaning, 'a watercourse, parts of which are situated in different states.'[41] This definition of a watercourse therefore embraces the interconnectivity of the *system* of waters that flow between states, while avoiding the 'basin'

34 Preamble, UN Watercourses Convention.

35 Comments and Observations Received from Governments, supra note 22. Canada, for example, suggested that, 'a framework of residual rules ... would be legally binding when watercourse States do not otherwise agree on a governing regime', supra note 22, at 149.

36 Rieu-Clarke, supra note 25, at 153–155.

37 Article 1 (1), UN Watercourses Convention.

38 The term 'drainage basin' had appeared in the International Law Association's, Helsinki Rules on the Uses of the Waters of International Rivers (Helsinki), which defined them as being, 'a geographical area extending over two or more states determined by the watershed limits of the system of waters, including surface and underground waters, flowing into a common terminus', see Helsinki Rules, in S. Bogdanović, *International Law of Water Resources* (London: Kluwer Law International 2001), 99–145, at 100.

39 Replies of Governments to the Commission's Questionnaire, UN Doc. A/CN.4/294 & Add. 1, supra note 22, at 162.

40 Article 2(a), UN Watercourses Convention. Given that Article 2(a) solely defines a 'watercourse' as being the water itself, it might be seen as slightly at odds with Article 1(1), of the UN Watercourses Convention, which refers to 'watercourses and ... their waters.'

41 Article 2(b), UN Watercourses Convention.

terminology that some states resisted. In addition, it can be argued that the protection, preservation and management of international watercourses, the key objective of the UN Watercourses Convention, would not be possible without taking into account both land- and water-related activities within a basin.

A drainage basin approach is also reflected in the main substantive norms of the UN Watercourses Convention. The overarching substantive requirement is that, 'Watercourse States shall in their respective territories utilize an international watercourse in an equitable and reasonable manner.'[42] In determining how to utilise an international watercourse in an equitable and reasonable manner, states are required to take into account all relevant factors and circumstances.[43] The Watercourses Convention does not stipulate the weight that should be given to different uses, but rather provides that, 'no use of an international watercourse enjoys inherent priority over other uses', and 'special regard' should be afforded to, 'the requirements of vital human needs.'[44]

A further qualification on the equitable and reasonable utilisation principle is set out in Article 7, which provides that, 'Watercourse States shall, in utilizing an international watercourse in their territories, take all appropriate measures to prevent the causing of significant harm to other watercourses States.'[45] Such a requirement is, however, aligned to the principle of equitable and reasonable utilisation in that, where significant harm is caused to another watercourse state, it will only be considered unlawful if it is also deemed to be contrary to the principle of equitable and reasonable utilisation.[46] While some writers have argued that this approach may favour socio-economic uses of international watercourses over those that are potentially harmful to the environment,[47] it should be remembered that the UN Watercourses Convention also stresses the importance of protecting the environment of international

42 Article 5(1), UN Watercourses Convention.

43 Art. 6, UN Watercourses Convention.

44 Art. 10, UN Watercourses Convention.

45 Art. 7.

46 Art. 7(2).

47 E. Hey, 'The Watercourses Convention: To What Extent Does it Provide a Basis for Regulating Uses on International Watercourses', 7 Review of European, Comparative & International Environmental Law (1998) 291–300; A. Nollkaemper, 'The Contribution of the International Law Commission to International Water Law: Does it Reverse the Flight from Substance?', 27 Netherlands Yearbook of International Law (1996) 39–73. See also Salman, supra note 29.

watercourses.[48] Article 20, for example, stipulates that, 'Watercourse States shall, individually and, where appropriate, jointly, protect and preserve ecosystems of international watercourses.'[49] Along similar lines, Article 5 of the Watercourses Convention states that any determination of equitable and reasonable utilisation should aim towards a sustainable utilisation of an international watercourse,[50] and watercourse states must cooperate in the protection of an international watercourse.[51] Such emphasis on environmental needs, and a growing scientific understanding and recognition of the importance of the need to protect the environment, suggests that environmental needs and interests may afford similar protection as the requirement to protect vital human needs in the determination of what is equitable and reasonable.[52]

In order to support the key substantive norms, the UN Watercourses Convention sets out a series of procedural requirements.[53] States are placed under an obligation to cooperate, 'on the basis of sovereign equality, territorial integrity, mutual benefit and good faith in order to attain optimal utilisation and adequate protection of an international watercourse.'[54] More specific procedural requirements are also included within the text, the most detailed

---

48 See generally, O. McIntyre, *Environmental Protection of International Watercourses under International Law* (London: Ashgate Publishing Group 2007); O. McIntyre, 'The Emergence of an "Ecosystem Approach" to the Protection of International Watercourses under International Law', 13(1) Review of European, Comparative & International Environmental Law (2004), 2–14; O. McIntyre, 'The Protection of Freshwater Ecosystems Revisted: Towards a Common Understanding of the "Ecosystems Approach" to the Protection of Transboundary Resources', 32(1) Review of European, Comparative & International Environmental Law (2014) 88–95; J. Lee, *Preservation of Ecosystems of International Watercourses and the Integration of Relevant Rules—An Interpretative Mechanism to Address the Fragmentation of International Law* (London: Brill 2014).

49 Art. 20. See also Art. 21 (Prevention, reduction and control of pollution), Art. 22 (Introduction of alien or new species), and Art. 23 (Protection and preservation of the marine environment).

50 Art. 5(1), UN Watercourses Convention.

51 Art. 5(2), UN Watercourses Convention.

52 Rieu-Clarke & Spray, 'Ecosystems Services and International Water Law: Towards a More Effective Determination and Implementation of Equity?'16(2) Potscheftstroom Electronic Review (2013) 12–65.

53 On the importance of procedural requirements, see O. McIntyre, 'The Proceduralisation and Growing Maturity of International Water Law: Case Concerning Pulp Mills on the River Uruguay (Argentina v. Uruguay), 22(3) Journal of Environmental Law (2010) 475–497.

54 Art. 8(1), UN Watercourses Convention.

of which relates to notification and consultation of planned measures.[55] Watercourses states are obligated to notify another state or states in a timely manner of any planned measures that may have a significant adverse effect on their uses of an international watercourse.[56] Notification must be accompanied by available technical data and information, including, where available, any environmental impact assessment that may have been conducted. The Convention goes on to set out additional detail concerning, *inter alia,* the time period for replying to a notification,[57] obligations upon states during the notifying period,[58] and procedures to follow in the absence of notification.[59]

As well as procedural requirements relating to the notification of planned measures, the UN Watercourses Convention also sets out additional procedural requirements. The Convention provides an explicit requirement for states to cooperate in the regular exchange of data and information and in relation to emergency situations.[60] Additional requirements to cooperate on procedural matters can be inferred from key provisions of the Watercourses Convention, such as the requirement to take 'all appropriate measures' to prevent significant harm.[61] This requirement, which is considered to be a due diligence obligation, might require states to put in place procedural frameworks pertaining to permitting and licensing, stakeholder participation, and environmental impact assessment.[62] Many other provisions of the UN Watercourses Convention, whilst not stipulating the detail, require states to, 'where appropriate, jointly', conduct certain actions, including: the prevention, reduction and control of pollution;[63] the protection and preservation of the marine environment;[64]

55 Art. 11. See also Art. 5(2), which obliges watercourse states to, 'cooperate in the protection and development' of an international watercourse.

56 Art. 12, UN Watercourses Convention.

57 Art. 13, UN Watercourses Convention.

58 Art. 14, UN Watercourses Convention.

59 Art. 18, UN Watercourses Convention.

60 Art. 9 and 26 of the UN Watercourses Convention.

61 Art. 7, UN Watercourses Convention.

62 See A. Tanzi, A. Kolliopoulos & N. Nikiforova, 'Normative Features of the UNECE Water Convention', in A. Tanzi, et al. (eds), *The UNECE Convention on the Protection and Use of Transboundary Watercourses and International Lakes: Its Contribution to International Water Cooperation* (London: Brill 2015), 116–129, at 122–128; UNECE, Guide to Implementing the Water Convention, 2013, UN Doc. ECE/MP.WAT/39, at 10–12.

63 Art. 21, UN Watercourses Convention.

64 Art. 23, UN Watercourses Convention.

regulation;[65] and the prevention and mitigation of harmful conditions.[66] Such cooperative efforts will more often than not be procedural in nature.

An additional mechanism envisaged in the UN Watercourses Convention to support the implementation of substantive norms relates to the establishment of institutional arrangements. While the Convention falls short of explicitly requiring watercourse states to establish joint institutional arrangements, states are obliged to, 'enter into consultations concerning the management of an international watercourse, which may include the establishment of a joint management mechanism.'[67]

Finally, a key feature of the UN Watercourses Convention is Article 33, which sets out a stepwise procedure by which states might settle any disputes in a peaceful manner. Initially, watercourse states are obliged to settle their disputes by negotiation.[68] Failing that, states, 'may jointly seek the good offices of, or request mediation or conciliation by, a third party, or make use, as appropriate, of any joint watercourse institutions that may have been established by them or agree to submit the dispute to arbitration or to the International Court of Justice.'[69] There is therefore considerable discretion as to the means by which states might choose to settle their dispute. However, if the dispute remains unresolved after six months, the dispute, at the request of one of the states, must be submitted to an impartial third-party fact-finding commission, which will investigate the dispute and provide a recommendation on how it might be resolved.[70] The parties must consider the recommendation of the third-party fact-finding commission in good faith.[71]

65 Art. 25, UN Watercourses Convention.

66 Art. 27, UN Watercourses Convention.

67 Art. 24 of the UN Watercourses Convention. Art. 8 also provides that, 'watercourse States may consider the establishment of joint mechanisms or commissions, as deemed necessary by them, to facilitate cooperation on relevant measures and procedures in the light of experience gained through cooperation in existing joint mechanisms and commission in various regions.'

68 Art. 33(1), UN Watercourses Convention.

69 Art. 33(2), UN Watercourses Convention.

70 Art. 33(2)-(7), UN Watercourses Convention.

71 Art. 33(8).

II *The UNECE Water Convention*

(a) Evolution and Status

The UNECE started working on water issues in the 1940s.[72] During this initial phase, the UNECE's activities related to water focused on issues of hydropower. For instance, UNECE played a role in the development of a bilateral agreement between Austria and Yugoslavia relating to the utilisation of the Drava River for the purposes of hydro-electric power generation.[73] By the 1960s, a UNECE Committee on Water Problems was established. Over the course of the next three decades, it produced a series of recommendations, declarations and decisions on water matters, including long-term planning for: water management; desalinisation; groundwater recharge; the use of economic instruments in water management; drinking water and sanitation; prevention and control of water pollution; international cooperation; waste-water treatment; and dam safety.[74]

---

72 A. Rieu-Clarke, 'Remarks on the Drafting History of the Convention' in A. Tanzi, *et al.* (eds), *The UNECE Convention on the Protection and Use of Transboundary Watercourses and International Lakes: Its Contribution to International Water Cooperation* (London: Brill 2015), 3–14; Y. Berthelot and P. Rayment, 'Looking Back and Peering Forward—A Short History of the United Nations Economic Commission for Europe', 1947–2007 (2007) UN Doc. ECE/INF/2007/4, at 33.

73 Convention between the Governments of the Federal People's Republic of Yugoslavia and the Federal Government of the Austrian Republic Concerning Water Economy Questions Relating to the Drava (1954).

74 See for example, UNECE, Declaration of Policy on Water Pollution Control, 29 April 1966, UN Doc. E/ECE/1084; UNECE, Recommendations to ECE Governments on Long-term Planning of Water Management, May 1976, UN Doc. ECE/ENVWA/2; UNECE, Recommendations to ECE Governments on Selected Water Problems in Islands and Coastal Areas with Special Regard to Desalination and Ground Water, December 1978, UN Doc. ECE/ENVWA/2; UNECE, Recommendations to ECE Governments on Rational Utilization of Water, December 1979, UN Doc. ECE/ENVWA/2; UNECE, Recommendations to ECE Governments on Economic Instruments for Rational Water Resources, December 1980, UN Doc. ECE/ENVWA/2; UNECE, Declaration of Policy on Prevention and Control of Water Pollution, including Transboundary Water Pollution, 1980, UN Doc. E/ECE/WATER/38; UNECE, Recommendations to ECE Governments on Water Pollution from Animal Production, December 1981, UN Doc. ECE/ENVWA/2; UNECE, Decision on International Co-operation on Shared Water Resources, December 1982, UN Doc. ECE/ENVWA/2; UNECE, Recommendations to ECE Governments on Drinking Water Supply and Effluent Disposal System, December 1982, UN Doc. ECE/ENVWA/2; UNECE, Declaration of Policy on the Rational Use of Water, December 1984, UN Doc. ECE/ENVWA/2; UNECE, Decision on Co-operation in the Field of Transboundary Waters, December 1986, UN Doc. ECE/WATER/42; UNECE, Recommendations to ECE Governments on Rational Use of Water in Industrial Processes, December 1987, UN Doc. ECE/ENVWA/2; UNECE,

In 1989 it was suggested that a framework instrument be concluded amongst the states of the UNECE region, which would in part consolidate and give legally binding effect to much of the aforementioned previous work that had been carried out in this area.[75] A meeting of the 'Senior Advisors to UNECE Governments' discussed this suggestion from 26 February to 2 March 1990.[76] A key outcome of the meeting was a recognition of the urgency of elaborating a framework convention.[77] Five special sessions of the UNECE Working Party on Water Problems took place between May 1990 and October 1991 in order to elaborate the text of the proposed Convention. These meetings involved representatives from a diverse group of 25 states, as well as several international organisations.[78] The outcome of the meetings, namely a draft Convention, was submitted to the fifth session of the Senior Advisors to UNECE Governments on Environmental and Water Problems, which was held on 20 March 1992. The draft Convention was subsequently adopted, and all UNECE states and regional economic integration organisations were encouraged to sign and ratify the instrument as soon as possible to ensure its prompt entry into force.[79] The drafting and the negotiation of the UNECE Water Convention was therefore considerably shorter than the UN Water Convention. A major factor

---

Recommendations to ECE Governments on Water-management Systems, 2 December 1987, UN Doc. ECE/ENVWA/2; UNECE, Recommendations to ECE Governments on Waste-water Treatment, March 1988, UN Doc. ECE/CEP/10; UNECE, Recommendations to ECE Governments on the Protection of Soil and Aquifers Against Non-point Source Pollution, March 1988, UN Doc. ECE/CEP/10; UNECE, Recommendations to ECE Governments on Dam Safety with Particular Emphasis on Small Dams, March 1989, UN Doc. ECE/CEP/10; UNECE, Charter on Ground-water Management, December 1989, UN Doc. ECE/ENVWA/12.

75 OSCE, 'Report on Conclusions and Recommendations of the Meeting on the Protection of the Environment of the Conference on Security and Co-operation in Europe', 5 November 1990, http://www.osce.org/eea/14075?download=true (accessed 24 November 2016).

76 UNECE, Senior Advisers to ECE Governments on Environmental and Water Problems—Report of the Third Session, 12 March 1990, UN Doc. ECE/ENVWA/14.

77 Ibid., at 5.

78 The following governments participated: Austria, Belgium, Bulgaria, Canada, Czech and Slovak Federal Republic, Denmark, Finland, France, German Democratic Republic, Federal Republic of Germany, Greece, Hungary, Italy, Netherlands, Norway, Poland, Portugal, Romania, Spain, Sweden, Switzerland, Turkey, Union of the Soviet Socialist Republics, United Kingdom, United States of America; together with the Food and Agricultural Organisation, the World Meteorological Organisation, the European Economic Community and the Danube Commission.

79 UNECE, Decision B(5) on the Convention on the Protection and Use of Transboundary Watercourses and International Lakes', in Report of fifth session.

that most likely assisted in the drafting and negotiation of the UNECE Water Convention was the existing work, spanning three decades, that the UNECE states had conducted together on matters relating to water. This groundwork most likely helped to settle major differences across a diverse region. After a relatively short period from its adoption, the UNECE Water Convention entered into force in 1996.[80] To date, 41 states are party to the UNECE Water Convention.[81]

The UNECE Water Convention has developed significantly since its entry into force in 1996. Two additional protocols have been negotiated under the Convention, one related to 'Water and Health',[82] and the other concerning 'Civil Liability and Compensation for Damage Caused by the Transboundary Effects of Industrial Accidents on Transboundary Waters.'[83] A series of recommendations, guidance notes and other publications have also been adopted by the parties of the UNECE Water Convention in order to strengthen its implementation.[84] However, the most significant development for the purposes of this monograph was the decision made by the parties of the UNECE Water Convention in 2003 to amend the Convention in order to allow accession by countries outside the UNECE region.[85] The amendment entered into force

80 The UNECE Water Convention entered into force on 6 October 1996, following the 16th instrument of ratification, acceptance, approval or accession (see Art. 26 of the UNECE Water Convention).

81 See UN Treaty Collection, https://treaties.un.org/Pages/ViewDetails.aspx?src=TREATY&mtdsg_no=XXVII-5&chapter=27&clang=_en (accessed 24 November 2016).

82 Protocol on Water and Health to the 1992 Convention on the Protection and Use of Transboundary Watercourses and International Lakes (1999).

83 Protocol on Civil Liability and Compensation for Damage Caused by the Transboundary Effects of Industrial Accidents on Transboundary Waters to the 1992 Convention on the Protection and Use of Transboundary Watercourses and International Lakes and to the 1992 Convention on the Transboundary Effects of Industrial Accidents (2003).

84 See for example UNECE, Policy Guidance Note on the Benefits of Transboundary Water Cooperation, October 2015, UN Doc. ECE/MP.WAT/47; UNECE, Model Provisions on Transboundary Groundwaters, February 2014, UN Doc. ECE/MP.WAT/40; Guide to Implementing the Water Convention, supra note 62; UNECE, Guidance on Water and Adaptation to Climate Change, October 2009, UN Doc. ECE/MP.WAT/30; UNECE, Recommendations on Payments for Ecosystem Services in Integrated Water Resources Management, August 2007, UN Doc. ECE/MP.WAT/22; Good Practice in Monitoring and Assessment of Transboundary Rivers, Lakes and Groundwaters, December 2006, UN Doc. ECE/ENHS/2006/18; and Guidelines on Sustainable Flood Management, January 2000, UN Doc. MP.WAT/2000/7.

85 Supra note 11.

in 2013 and became operational in March 2016.[86] This opens up the possibility for Mekong states, along with other countries around the world, to join the UNECE Water Convention.

(b) Overview

The primary objective of the UNECE Water Convention, as set out in its title and preamble, is the protection and use of transboundary watercourses and international lakes. In the operational part of the Convention, 'transboundary watercourses' and 'international lakes' are conflated into the term 'transboundary waters', which is defined as being, 'any surface or ground waters which mark, cross or are located on boundaries between two or more States.'[87] Groundwater that is both connected or unconnected to surface water therefore falls within the scope of the UNECE Water Convention.

As a framework instrument, the UNECE Water Convention obliges states to, 'enter into bilateral or multilateral agreements or other arrangements, where these do not yet exist, or adapt existing ones, where necessary, to eliminate the contradictions with the basic principles of' the Convention.'[88] What constitutes 'the basic principles' of the UNECE Water Convention are not spelled out in the agreement, but the use of such a term would suggest there is considerable flexibility in how existing agreements might be viewed alongside this framework instrument.[89]

The main substantive obligations of the UNECE Water Convention are set out in Articles 2 and 3. Article 2(1) requires parties to 'take all appropriate measures to prevent, control and reduce transboundary impact.' What constitutes 'transboundary impact' is defined broadly to mean, 'any significant

---

86 Supra note 12.

87 Art. 1(1), UNECE Water Convention. Art. 1(1) goes on to explain that, 'wherever transboundary waters flow directly into the sea, these transboundary waters end at a straight line across their respective mouths between points on the low-water of their banks.'

88 Art. 9(1), UNECE Water Convention.

89 The UNECE, Guide to Implementing the Water Convention (supra note 62, at 64), suggests that:

> "The reference to 'basic principles' should not be read in a restrictive manner, so as to refer only to those provisions which coincide with the recognized principles of international environmental law. Such reference should be read in line with the ordinary meaning of its wording to the effect that the pre-existing water agreements between the Riparian parties do not contravene the fundamental provisions of the Convention itself. At the same time, reference to the "basic principles" of the Convention avoids the requirement to incorporate every single provision of the Convention in case there is a need to adapt existing agreements to the Convention."

adverse effect on the environment resulting from a change in the conditions of transboundary waters caused by a human activity, the physical origin of which is situated wholly or in part within an area under the jurisdiction of a Party, within an area under the jurisdiction of another Party.'[90] The Article goes on to explain that, 'such effects on the environment include effects on human health and safety, flora, fauna, soil, air, water, climate, landscape, and historical monuments or other physical structures or the interaction among these factors; they also include effects on the cultural heritage or socio-economic conditions resulting from alternations to those factors.'[91]

While such effects might appear wide-ranging, it is important to bear in mind that in practice what will be required by states will depend on the nature and risk of any potential transboundary impact and the capacity of states to prevent, control and reduce such impact.[92] In determining what measures might be appropriate, states are further guided that they: prevent, control and reduce pollution of waters causing or likely to cause transboundary impact; ensure that transboundary waters are used with the aim of ecologically sound and rational water management, conservation of water resources and environmental protection; ensure that transboundary waters are used in a reasonable and equitable way, taking into particular account their transboundary character, in the case of activities which cause or are likely to cause transboundary impact; ensure conservation and, where necessary, restoration of ecosystems.[93] Additionally, in taking the appropriate measures to prevent, control and reduce transboundary impact, states must be guided by the precautionary principle, the polluter-pays principle and the principle of inter-generational equity.[94]

The UNECE Water Convention recognises the importance of procedure in implementing the aforementioned substantive rights and obligations. States are obliged to adopt several legal, administrative, financial and technical measures to prevent, control and reduce transboundary impact.[95] Such measures include: the use of low- and non-waste technology in the prevention, control and reduction of the emission of pollutants; the protection of pollution at source through waste-water discharges, which should be monitored and controlled; placing limits on waste-water discharges based on the best available technology for discharges of hazardous substances; the adoption of stricter

90 Art. 1(2), UNECE Water Convention.

91 Ibid.

92 See Tanzi et al., supra note 62.

93 Art. 2(2), UNECE Water Convention.

94 Art. 2(5), UNECE Water Convention.

95 Art. 3(1), UNECE Water Convention.

requirements, even leading to prohibition, when the quality of the receiving water or the ecosystem so requires; the adoption of at least biological treatment or equivalent processes for municipal waste water; the application of best available technology to reduce nutrient inputs from industrial and municipal sources; the development and implementation of best environmental practices for the reduction of inputs of nutrients and hazardous substances from diffuse sources; the application of environmental impact assessment and other means of assessment; the promotion of sustainable water-resources management, including the ecosystem approach; the development of contingency planning; the taking of specific measures to prevent groundwater from pollution; and the minimization of risk of accidental pollution.[96]

Additional procedural requirements set out in the UNECE Water Convention include: requirements to enter into consultations;[97] monitor the conditions of transboundary water;[98] cooperate in the carrying out of research and development;[99] the exchange of data and information;[100] and the provision of public information regarding, 'the conditions of transboundary waters, measures taken or planned to be taken to prevent, control and reduce transboundary impact, and the effectiveness of those measures.'[101]

Implementation of the provisions of the UNECE Water Convention is supported through a strong emphasis on institutional arrangements. At the level of individual transboundary waters, states are obligated to: establish 'joint bodies', which are required to carry out a range of functions, including the identification of pollution sources likely to cause transboundary impact, the elaboration of joint monitoring programmes, the development of inventories and exchange information on pollution sources; the elaboration of emission limits for wastewater; the elaboration of joint water-quality objectives and criteria; the development of joint action programmes for the reduction of pollution loads from point and diffuse pollution sources; the establishment of warning and alarm procedures. States must also: act as a forum for the exchange of information on existing and planned uses of water and related installations that are likely to cause transboundary impact; promote cooperation and exchange of information on best available technology; and participate

96 Art. 3(1), UNECE Water Convention.
97 Art. 10, UNECE Water Convention.
98 Arts. 4 & 11, UNECE Water Convention.
99 Arts. 5 & 12, UNECE Water Convention.
100 Arts. 6 & 13, UNECE Water Convention.
101 Art. 16, UNECE Water Convention.

in the implementation of environmental impact assessments relating to transboundary waters.[102]

As well as putting in place institutional arrangements at the level of specific transboundary waters, the UNECE Water Convention also provides for the establishment of an overarching institutional framework to support the implementation and development of the Convention.[103] A meeting of the parties is to be convened every three years in order to review the policies and methodologies that have been adopted to: support the implementation of the Convention; to exchange information on experiences gained in the implementation of the Convention; to seek services of relevant ECE bodies and other competent international bodies in support of the Convention; and consider and adopt proposals for amendments to the Convention.[104] The Convention also establishes a secretariat, which functions include: convening and preparing meetings of the parties; transmitting reports and other information related to the Convention to the parties; and any other activities that the parties deem appropriate.[105]

Finally, the UNECE Water Convention provides certain dispute-settlement mechanisms. In the first instance, parties are obliged to seek to resolve their disputes by negotiation, or any other means acceptable to the parties.[106] Parties are also encouraged, upon signing, ratifying, accepting, approving or acceding to the Convention, to declare in writing that for any disputes that are not resolved by negotiation of other means, that they accept to submit the dispute to compulsory dispute settlement either by the International Court of Justice (ICJ) or arbitration.[107]

III *Joint Promotion of Both Conventions*

Given that states now have the option to join both the UN Watercourses Convention and the UNECE Water Convention, a concerted effort has been undertaken to ascertain and promote the benefits of both conventions.

Studies that have compared the two conventions have led to the conclusion that they are compatible with each other.[108] Such a finding of compatibility

102 Art. 9(2), UNECE Water Convention.

103 Part III, UNECE Water Convention.

104 Art. 17, UNECE Water Convention.

105 Art. 19, UNECE Water Convention.

106 Art. 22(1), UN Water Convention.

107 Art. 22(2) & Annex IV, UNECE Water Convention.

108 See for example, UNECE, The Economic Commission for Europe Water Convention and the United Nations Watercourses Convention—An Analysis of their Harmonized Contribution to International Water Law, 2015, UN Doc. ECE/MP.WAT.42.

is consistent with the principle of harmonisation in international law, which stipulates that, 'when several norms bear on a single issue they should, to the extent possible, be interpreted so as to give rise to a single set of compatible obligations.'[109] This is not to say that the conventions are exactly the same. Far from it. While core principles are shared between the two instruments, there are some significant differences in the text. Where one convention provides a general provision on a particular matter, the other convention may go into more detail. Examples can be seen through the comparative analysis of the two conventions, and the Mekong Agreement, which will be conducted below. However, it is important to note here that these differences justify supporting the promotion of both conventions as a fuller package of legal norms relating to international watercourses.

The need to promote both conventions as a package has been gaining increasing momentum in recent years. For instance, at the 6th session of the Meeting of the Parties to the UNECE Water Convention, the UN Secretary-General stated that, '[t]he globalisation of the UNECE Convention should also go hand-in-hand with the expected entry into force of the Watercourses Convention. These two instruments are based on the same principles. They complement each other and should be implemented in a coherent manner.'[110] The complementary nature of the two conventions is also reflected by the number of states that have become a party to both instruments, which include Denmark, Finland, France, Germany, Greece, Hungary, Italy, Luxembourg, Montenegro, Netherlands, Norway, Portugal, Spain and Sweden.

Various activities and studies have also sought to explore how the international community might best capitalise upon the synergies between the two instruments. For example, the current work programme of the UNECE Water Convention stipulates that:

> The Meeting of the Parties will promote synergies and coordination with the Watercourses Convention by sharing the experience collected under the Water Convention to support the implementation of the Watercourses Convention, promoting exchanges and ordination between

---

109 UN General Assembly, Report of the International Law Commission 48th Session, 2006, UN Doc. A/61/10, at 408.

110 UN Secretary-General, Message to Meeting of Parties to the United Nations Economic Commission for Europe (UNECE) Convention on the Protection and Use of Transboundary Watercourses and International Lakes, https://www.unece.org/fileadmin/DAM/env/water/mop_6_Rome/Presentations/Secretary_General_message.pdf (accessed 24 November 2012).

> the parties to the two Conventions and by offering an intergovernmental framework for discussion and provision of information on the two Conventions.[111]

Pursuant to this ambition, a range of activities have been organised in order to raise awareness to the two water conventions, and assess their relevance within specific regions and countries.[112] These workshops have been complemented by activities that have taken place at a global level to promote the two water conventions in tandem.[113]

Promotion of the two water conventions in tandem requires effective coordination. Currently, there is only an informal arrangement in support of the UN Watercourses Convention, whereas the UNECE Water Convention is supported by the aforementioned institutional framework, which includes a Meeting of the Parties and Secretariat.[114] As both conventions evolve and support for them gathers pace, it will be important to put in place effective institutional arrangements that can maximise the synergies between both instruments.[115]

---

111 UNECE, Report of the Meeting of the Parties on its Seventh Session, 7 July 2016, UN Doc. ECE/MP.WAT/49/Add.1, at 13.

112 Such activities include workshops that have explored the relevance of the two Conventions within particular regions, including the Workshop on Transboundary Water Cooperation in Latin America and Pan European Regions, 11–12 June 2013, Buenos Aires, Argentina; the Workshop on General Principles of Transboundary Water Cooperation, 3–4 October 2016, Campeche, Mexico; a side event on International Water Law at the Sixth Africa Water Week, 18–22 July 2016, Dar es Salaam, Tanzania; National Workshop on the UNECE Water Convention: Key Aspects and Opportunities for Iraq, 13–14 January 2016, Amman, Jordan; National Workshop on Frameworks for Transboundary Water Cooperation: Focus on the UNECE Water Convention, 10 March 2015, Amman, Jordan; Workshop on the UNECE Water Convention: Key Aspects and Opportunities for Lebanon, 4–5 February, Beirut, Lebanon; workshop on Legal Frameworks for Cooperation on Transboundary Waters—Key Aspects and Opportunities for the Arab Countries, 11–12 June 2014.

113 See for example a side event on 'The Surprising Benefits of Transboundary Water Cooperation', organised at the Stockholm World Water Week, 28 August, 2016; and a Special Focus Session at the World Water Forum on 'Two Global Conventions on Transboundary Water Cooperation: So What?' 14 April 2015, Daegu, Republic of Korea.

114 See generally, A. Rieu-Clarke & R. Kinna, 'Can Two Global UN Water Conventions Effectively Co-exist? Making the Case for a 'Package Approach' to Support Institutional Coordination', 23(1) Review of European, Comparative & International Environmental Law (2014) 15–31.

115 Ibid.

IV *Evolution, Overview and Status of the Mekong Agreement*

(a) Key Characteristics

The unique nature of the Mekong River Basin, its hydro-geographical features, the people who live there, and the resources and ecosystems upon which they rely has dictated the evolution of cooperation within the basin. Originating high within the Tibetan Plateau and making its way down through China, Myanmar, Laos, Thailand, Cambodia and finally Vietnam, where it forms the Mekong Delta and empties into the South China Sea, the Mekong River is a uniquely inter-connected and hydro-geographical resource.[116] That the river flows down from approximately 5,000 metres above sea level in Tibet is a critical point to highlight, because this steepness of decline in the run of the river is what provides the potential for hydropower development.[117] The river itself is 4,800 kilometres long and the basin encompasses an area of 795,000 square kilometres, making it the 21st largest river basin in the world.[118] In terms of approximate area per basin state: 20 percent falls inside China's borders, three percent within Myanmar, 25 percent in Laos, 20 percent in Thailand, 19 percent in Cambodia and eight percent within Vietnam.[119] The relative position of each riparian along the mainstream of the River had, and still has, extremely crucial implications for the role of each state in the negotiation, development and membership of the Mekong Agreement and MRC.

In hydrological terms, the Mekong River is divided into two very distinguishable sub-basins: the Upper Mekong Basin, incorporating the head of the River and narrow upstream highland areas within China and Myanmar; and the Lower Mekong Basin, encompassing the lower half of the river's length yet the majority—roughly three quarters—of its lowland catchment area across Laos, Thailand, Cambodia and Vietnam.[120] Notably for the purposes of this monograph, the dichotomy between the Upper and Lower Mekong Basins is often a commonly referred to delineation not only in a hydro-geographical sense, but also from a hydro-political and governance sense as the Upper

116 MRC, *State of the Basin Report 2010* (Vientiane: MRC 2010).

117 N. Van Duyen, 'The Inadequacies of Environmental Protection Mechanisms in the Mekong River Basin Agreement 6 Asia Pacific Journal of Environmental Law (2001) 349–376, at 350; ICEM, *MRC Strategic Environmental Assessment (SEA) of Hydropower on the Mekong Mainstream: Summary of the Final Project* (Hanoi: MRC 2010).

118 MRC, supra note 116.

119 Food and Agriculture Organisation, 'Aquastat—Mekong River Basin' http://www.fao.org/nr/water/aquastat/basins/mekong/index.stm (accessed 24 November 2016).

120 B. Bearden, A. Rieu-Clarke & S. Pech, 'Mekong Basin', in F. Rocha Loures & A. Rieu-Clarke (eds.), *The UN Watercourses Convention in Force—Strengthening International Law for Transboundary Water Management* (Abingdon: Routledge 2013) 180–188, at 181.

Mekong Basin states are not party to the Mekong Agreement nor the MRC.[121] However, one must be careful in drawing reference to these two distinct basins in the context of the regional legal, political and geographic landscape, as conflations or extrapolations on the basis of hydrological catchments can oversimplify or confuse matters. Moreover, there are significant contrasting elements between states within both sub-basins, including 'vast differences between the four lower Mekong countries in terms of geography, population size and level of economic development.'[122]

Tributaries play a vital role within the Mekong River basin, more so than many other rivers. The entire Mekong drainage network is extremely complex, with the Lower Mekong Basin alone comprising more than 100 major and minor tributaries, some of which are transboundary in nature.[123] What is most critical about these tributaries is their significant yet vastly uneven contribution to the flow of the Mekong River mainstream. On average, tributaries provide over 44 of flow to the Mekong.[124] This disproportionately high volumetric input by tributaries into the mainstream flow regime is only matched in extremes by their fluctuation according to tropical monsoonal seasons. There is an enormous increase in flow of the Mekong from tributaries throughout the wet season, which traditionally lasts from around May until December and results in massive flooding of the Lower Mekong Basin. In turn, this flooding supports, 'a productive and diverse freshwater ecosystem', although it can, 'also result in loss of human life and damage to crops and structures.'[125] Such an abundance of water can be contrasted with the dry season that commences in December, when flows traditionally begin to recede and eventually reach their lowest levels in April. As Paisley highlights, the 'dramatic reduction of flow leads to water shortages for domestic and agricultural use' whereby, '[e]quitable sharing of the water resources and sustainable development of the natural resources in the basin becomes most critical for each country.'[126]

121 M. Osborne, *River at Risk: The Mekong and Water Politics of China and Southeast Asia* (London: Longueville Media 2004); E. Goh, *Developing the Mekong: Regionalism and Regional Security in China-Southeast Asian Relations* (Routledge, Abingdon 2007).

122 R. Paisley, 'Adversaries into Partners: International Water Law and the Equitable Sharing of Downstream Benefits', 3(2) Melbourne Journal of International Law (2002) 280–301, at 295.

123 MRC, The Flow of the Mekong (Vientiane: MRC 2009), at 4.

124 O. Toda, et al., 'Evaluation of Tributaries Contribution in the Mekong River Basin During Rainy and Dry Season', Proceedings of the 2nd Conference of the Asia Pacific Association of Hydrology and Water Resources, 239–248, 2004, Singapore.

125 Paisley, supra note 122.

126 Paisley, supra note 122.

A major challenge, which will be considered below, is how the legal framework relating to the Mekong can account for these basin characteristics.

However, prior to exploring the evolution of cooperative legal arrangements relating to the Mekong, it is important to also recognise two other natural phenomena of the basin, namely the the Tonlé Sap Lake in Cambodia and the Mekong Delta in Vietnam.

The Tonlé Sap is the largest freshwater lake in South East Asia and is a designated UNESCO Biosphere Reserve.[127] The flow dynamics of the basin, as discussed above, dramatically affect the lake in so far as the vast differences in seasonal flows change the direction of the flow between the lake and the Mekong mainstream depending on whether it is the wet (flows from the mainstream into the lake) or dry season (flows from the lake into the mainstream and thus dramatically shrinks the lake). Crucially, in terms of ecosystems and livelihoods, it is one of the most productive inland fisheries in the world.[128] Collectively, the fish in the Tonlé Sap Lake and the Mekong provide 80 percent of dietary protein for millions of Cambodians and Vietnamese.[129] An important component in sustaining such fish stocks is their ability to migrate up and down the Mekong and its tributaries in accordance with the wet and dry seasons.[130]

A further vital part of the Mekong's ecosystem in terms of sustaining livelihoods is the Mekong Delta in Vietnam, which accounts for approximately 20 percent of that country's total land area and supplies more than 50 percent of staple food.[131] Consequently, the delta is often referred to as the 'rice basket' of Vietnam because its floodplains feed a large proportion of people living in the Lower Mekong Basin and in turn makes Vietnam "the second largest rice

127 D. Lamberts, 'The Tonle Sap Lake as a Productive Ecosystem', 22(3) Water Resources Development (2006) 481–495.

128 N. Bonheur & B.D. Lane, 'Natural Resources Management for Human Security in Cambodia's Tonle Sap Biosphere Reserve', 5(1) Environmental Science & Policy (2002) 33–41.

129 G. Kite, *Developing a Hydrological Model for the Mekong Basin—Impacts of Basin Development on Fisheries Productivity* (Colombo: IWMI 2000), at 2.

130 P.J. Dugan, et al., 'Fish Migration, Dams, and Loss of Ecosystem Services in the Mekong Basin', 39(4) AMBIO (2010), 344–348; MRC, Fish Migrations of the Lower Mekong River Basin: Implications for Development, Planning and Environmental Management (Phnom Penh: MRC 2002).

131 M. Garschagen, et al., 'Socio-Economic Development in the Mekong Delta: Between the Prospects for Progress and the Realms of Reality', in F.G. Renaud & C. Kuenzer (eds.), *The Mekong Delta System: Interdisciplinary Analyses of a River Delta* (Dordrecht: Springer 2012).

exporting country in the world."[132] The productivity of the delta is heavily reliant not only on the waters flowing from the upstream of the Mekong, but also the transfer of sedimentation.[133]

Taken together, the Tonlé Sap and Mekong Delta form two distinct, naturally occurring aquatic ecosystems along the Mekong River and its tributaries; their water- and land-based resources have collectively supported countless generations of people living within this basin. The continued health and vitality of these finely balanced aquatic and terrestrial ecosystems is not only essential to the survival of all flora and fauna within these environments, but the daily survival and prosperity of most people across the region. It is within this unique geographical context that the Mekong Agreement and MRC evolved.

(b) Evolution and Status

Transboundary water cooperation in the Mekong River can be traced back to the early 1950s when Cambodia, Laos, Thailand and South Vietnam established the Mekong Committee.[134] Following the establishment of Mekong Committee, four distinct temporal periods in the cooperative governance of the Mekong can be identified. These four periods reflect a distinct legal framework that was developed and adapted in response to change in the geopolitical and socio-economic context within the basin as well as the interests of its states.[135]

However, prior to this initial commencement of substantial cooperative efforts between the basin state, the nature of interaction between populations living along the Mekong's mainstream and tributaries was characterised by war and conflict.[136] Conflict between different basin states had for decades ruled out any meaningful attempts at basin-wide cooperation, let alone the creation of a legal instrument by which to govern development on the Mekong and its tributaries.[137]

---

132 Van Duyen, supra note 117, at 350.

133 D.E. Walling, 'The Changing Sediment Load of the Mekong River', 37(3) AMBIO (2008) 150–157.

134 T. Myint, 'Democracy in Global Environmental Governance: Issues, Interests, and Actors in the Mekong and the Rhine', 10(1) Indiana Journal of Global Legal Studies (2003) 287–314.

135 B.L. Bearden, 'The Legal Regime of the Mekong River: A Look Back and Some Proposals for the Way Ahead', 12 Water Policy (2010) 798–821, at 800.

136 Van Duyen, supra note 117, at 353.

137 P. Hirsh, 'Beyond the Nation State: Natural Resource Conflict and National Interest in Mekong Hydropower Development', 29(3) Golden Gate University Law Review (1999) 399–414.

The outset of basin cooperation from 1957 to 1975 was dominated by the UN-facilitated formation of the Committee for the Coordination of Investigations of the Lower Mekong Basin (Mekong Committee) under the provisions of the 1957 Mekong Statute.[138] Comprising the governments of Cambodia, Laos, South Vietnam and Thailand, the Mekong Committee's mandate, as per Article 4 of the Statute, was to 'promote, coordinate, supervise and control the planning and investigation of water resources development projects.'[139] The committee 'developed as its centerpiece a plan for a Mekong cascade of large dams and reservoirs on the river's mainstream, the impetus of which was strong US influence.'[140]

The period 1975 to 1978 was characterized by renewed conflict and political changes within the region, highlighted by Cambodia leaving the existing framework for basin cooperation.[141] Although the Mekong Committee was suspended as a result of ongoing tensions during this period, in 1975 the basin states concluded the Joint Declaration of Principles for the Utilisation of the Waters of the Lower Mekong Basin (Joint Declaration).[142] Influenced in part by the globally recognized Helsinki Rules,[143] this Declaration was considered to be 'a milestone in the evolution of the Mekong regime.'[144] Crucially, the Joint Declaration incorporated the cornerstone concepts of international water law, such as equitable and reasonable utilisation,[145] the conservation of the basin, and pollution prevention. Additionally, 'major' tributaries were treated as part of the mainstream waters where dam developments were concerned.[146] In line

138 Statute of the Committee for Co-ordination of Investigations of Lower Mekong Basin (1957).

139 Ibid.

140 Bearden, supra note 135, at 800–801.

141 G. Browder & L. Ortolano, 'The Evolution of an International Water Resources Management Regime in the Mekong River Basin' 40 Natural Resources Journal 499–531, at 508–509.

142 Joint Declaration of Principles for Utilisation of the Waters of the Lower Mekong Basin (1975).

143 Supra note 38.

144 Browder & Ortolano, supra note 141, at 509.

145 Art. V reads: 'Individual projects on the Mainstream shall be planned and implemented in a manner conducive to the system development of the Basin's water resources, in the beneficial use of which each Basin State shall be entitled, within its territory, to a reasonable and equitable share.'

146 Art. XXI stipulates that, '[a] tributary recognised by all Basin States as a Major Tributary shall be considered as an integral part of the Basin development system and shall be governed by the provisions of the present Declaration of Principles applicable to the Mainstream.'

with the previous arrangements, all projects on the mainstream and tributaries required the express prior approval of all the basin states.[147]

In 1978, given the abeyance of the Mekong Committee, Thailand, Laos and Vietnam established the Interim Mekong Committee.[148] As a basin institution, it held an interim status because Cambodia at that time chose not to participate. However, the other lower Mekong states proceeded with cooperative efforts in the hope that Cambodia would later re-join.[149] What followed was an extended period of stasis during the 1980s. This period witnessed renewed nationalism and conflicts, coupled with China's unilateral plans for a series of cascade hydropower dams at the head of the river in Yunnan province.[150] With basin cooperation seemingly at a halt, the Interim Mekong committee disbanded in 1992.[151]

In stark contrast to the reign of the Interim Mekong Committee, there was a significant and rapid regional rapprochement during the early 1990s. This rapprochement reinvigorated basin-wide cooperation and attempted to codify a legal instrument for governance of the Mekong River.[152] In parallel, crucial economic changes occurred, especially the opening of the national economies in the Lower Mekong Basin to overseas markets and investment, which hastened the impetus for re-establishing cooperative efforts to govern transboundary water resources.[153] By now, significant overseas interests had entered the region seeking to capitalize on this development-oriented and relatively stable geo-political climate in order to fund large-scale national hydropower projects along the Mekong River mainstream and, to a lesser extent, but no less importantly, also on some tributaries.[154] This revitalized sense of regional cooperation for development, commonly referred to as the 'Mekong Spirit', is

---

147 Art. XX stipulates that, '[e]xtra-basin diversion of mainstream waters by a riparian State shall require the agreement of all Basin States.'

148 N. Mirumachi, *Transboundary Water Politics in the Developing World* (Abingdon: Routledge 2015), at 112.

149 Bearden, supra note 135, at 803.

150 F. Urban, et al., 'An Analysis of China's Investment in the Hydropower Sector in the Greater Mekong Sub-Region', 15(2) Environment, Development and Sustainability (2013) 301–324.

151 Mirumachi, supra note 148.

152 Hirsch, supra note 137, at 404.

153 Paisley, supra note 122, at 296.

154 C. Middleton, J. Garcia & T. Foran, 'Old and New Hydropower Players in the Mekong Region: Agendas and Strategies', in F. Molle, T. Foran & M. Käkönen, *Contested Waterscapes in the Mekong Region—Hydropower, Livelihoods and Governance* (London, Earthscan 2009) 23–54, at 26–29.

oft acknowledged as one of the main reasons underpinning the creation of the Mekong Agreement.[155]

Following Cambodia's request in 1991 to re-join cooperative negotiations, the Mekong Working Group was set up by the four lower Mekong states in order to develop a cooperative framework for the basin.[156] The Mekong Working Group, with the assistance of the UN, initiated several rounds of closed-door negotiations between Thailand, Laos, Vietnam and Cambodia which, at its last meeting in November 1994, culminated in the production of a Draft Agreement on Cooperation for the Sustainable Development of the Mekong River Basin.[157] Signed on 5 April 1995, the Mekong Agreement was consequently adopted and resulted in the establishment of the MRC, thereby replacing the Interim Mekong Committee. This milestone event heralded the dawn of a new era in regional cooperation and the formation of the Mekong River Basin's current legal framework.

(c) Overview

The 1995 Mekong Agreement is divided into six chapters and 42 articles. The objective of the Agreement is to foster cooperation,

> ... in all fields of sustainable development, utilisation, management and conservation of the water and related resources of the Mekong River Basin including, but not limited to irrigation, hydro-power, navigation, flood control, fisheries, timber floating, recreation and tourism, in a manner to optimise the multiple-use and mutual benefits of all riparians and to minimise the harmful effects that might result from natural occurrences and man-made activities.[158]

There is an inherent paradox in the objective of the Mekong Agreement. While the agreement adopts a basin approach, it was only the four lower Mekong states (Cambodia, Laos, Thailand and Vietnam) that negotiated and adopted the instrument. It might therefore be questioned whether the overarching objective of the agreement can ever be attained without formal endorsement

155 Bearden, supra note 135, at 800.

156 G. Browder, 'An Analysis of the Negotiations for the 1995 Mekong Agreement', 5(2) International Negotiations (2000) 237–261.

157 Radosevich & Olson, supra note 3.

158 Art. 1, Mekong Agreement.

by the two upper Mekong states of China and Myanmar—particularly in light of China's significant developments along the upper reaches of the river.[159]

In terms of substantive norms, and no doubt influenced by the work of the ILC on the law of the non-national uses of international watercourses, the Mekong Agreement sets out an obligation upon its parties to, 'utilise the waters of the Mekong River system in a reasonable and equitable manner in their respective territories, pursuant to all relevant factors and circumstances.'[160] This cornerstone principle of equitable and reasonable utilisation is supplemented by an obligation upon parties to, 'make every effort to avoid, minimize and mitigate harmful effects that might occur to the environment, especially the water quantity and quality, the aquatic (eco-system) conditions, and ecological balance of the river system, from the development and use of the Mekong River Basin water resources or discharge of wastes and return flows.'[161] The agreement goes on to provide that where harmful effects do cause substantial damage, the parties concerned should, 'determine all relative factors, the cause, extent of damage and responsibility for damages caused by that state in conformity with the principles of international law relating to state responsibility.'[162] More broadly, the Mekong Agreement also places its parties under a substantive obligation to, 'protect the environment, natural resources, aquatic life and conditions, and ecological balance of the Mekong River Basin from pollution or other harmful effects resulting from any development plans and uses of water and related resources in the Basin.'[163]

The main procedural provisions of the Mekong Agreement relate to planned uses. A tiered system of notification, consultation and agreement is set out in the Agreement. The lower threshold of notification[164] is required for intra-basin and inter-basin diversions on the tributaries of the Mekong,[165] as well as intra-basin uses on the mainstream of the Mekong River during the wet season.[166] On the mainstream of the river, a middle threshold of prior

159 M. Keskinen, K. Mehtonen & O. Varis, 'Transboundary Cooperation vs. Internal Ambitions: The Role of China and Cambodia in the Mekong Region', in I. Nevelina, et al. (eds), *International Water Security: Domestic Threats and Opportunities* (Tokyo: UN University Press 2008) 79–109.

160 Art. 5, Mekong Agreement.

161 Art. 7, Mekong Agreement.

162 Art. 8, Mekong Agreement.

163 Art. 3, Mekong Agreement.

164 'Notification' is defined in Chapter II of the Mekong Agreement as meaning: 'Timely providing information by a riparian to the Joint Committee on its Proposed use of water.'

165 Art. 5(A), Mekong Agreement.

166 Art. 5(B)(1)(a), Mekong Agreement.

consultation[167] is required for inter-basin diversions during the wet season and an intra-basin diversion during the dry-season. Finally, inter-basin diversion projects on the mainstream of the river during the dry season are subject to agreement by all parties.[168]

The Mekong Agreement also sets out the institutional framework that is designed to support its implementation. As originally envisaged, the MRC was the most publicized cooperative transboundary basin institution in the world, and it was proclaimed as a fundamental step towards overcoming the regional antagonisms of the past.[169] The MRC is comprised of a Council, Joint Committee and Secretariat.[170] The primary decision-making body is the Council, which meets in regular session once a year, and is made up of one member from each party who should be at ministerial or cabinet level.[171] Decisions of the Council are to be made by unanimous vote unless agreed otherwise.[172] The Council is supported by the Joint Committee, which meets in regular session twice a year, and is made up of one member from each party who should be 'no less than Head of Department level.'[173] The primary function of the Joint Committee is to oversee and monitor the implementation of the decisions made by the MRC Council. Additionally, the MRC is comprised of a secretariat that provides 'technical and administrative services' to the Council and the Joint Committee.[174]

Outside these three institutional pillars, the National Mekong Committees (NMCs) perform a vital but often-overlooked role by linking government departments to the main MRC structure and functions. The NMCs consequently coordinate MRC programs at the national level through NMC Secretariats in each country, and they provide links between the MRC Secretariat and the

167 'Prior consultation' is defined in Chapter II of the Agreement as meaning: 'Timely notification plus additional data and information to the Joint Committee as provided in the Rules for Water Utilisation and Inter-Basin Diversion under Article 26, that would allow the other member riparians to discuss and evaluate the impact of the Proposed Use upon their uses of water and any other effects, which is the basis for arriving at an agreement. Prior consultation is neither a right to veto the use nor unilateral right to use water by any riparian without taking into account other riparians' rights.'

168 Art. 5(B)(2)(b), Mekong Agreement.

169 J.W. Jacobs, 'The Mekong River Commission: Transboundary Water Resources Planning and Regional Security', 168(4) The Geographical Journal (2002) 354–364, at 354. Sneddon & Fox, supra note 5, at 184.

170 Art. 12, Mekong Agreement.

171 Arts. 15 & 17, Mekong Agreement.

172 Art. 20, Mekong Agreement.

173 Art. 21 & 23, Mekong Agreement.

174 Art. 28, Mekong Agreement.

appropriate national ministries and line agencies.[175] The specific organization and structure of the NMCs is left to the discretion of the respective states, and according to Hirsch, '[t]he technical and political strengths of the NMCs vary from one riparian to another.'[176]

According to its Mission Statement, the over-arching mandate of the MRC is 'to promote and coordinate sustainable management and development of water and related resources for the countries' mutual benefit and the people's well-being.'[177] The MRC's primary role is therefore one of coordination and fostering cooperation between member states via joint initiatives and policy measures. In considering the reach of the MRC, as provided for under the MRC, it is important to note that its decision-making and executive power is constrained. As Osborne points out, 'the MRC is a "creature" of the governments that are members of the Commission. While its critics might want it to be otherwise, the MRC has no mandate to act on its own in any fashion that has not been approved by the member countries.'[178] This places a critical limitation on the powers of the MRC whereby 'diplomacy, negotiation, and persuasion are the main tools at its disposal. As such, although the MRC was established by a formal Agreement, it is still largely depending upon the goodwill of its member States.'[179]

It is perhaps due to this limitation that the technical and scientific aspects of the MRC's work have received the majority of attention, as well as funding from external donors. This has resulted in the compilation of invaluable and extensive databases of information pertaining to key aspects such as hydrology, geography and fisheries covering both the basin as a whole as well as specific states and areas therein.[180] Indeed, some scientific studies have been ongoing to the extent that, '[s]ince 1995, donors have invested substantially in fisheries

175 P. Hirsch, 'Water Governance and Catchment Management in the Mekong Region', 15(2) The Journal of Environment & Development', (2006) 184–201, at 192.

176 Ibid.

177 MRC, Vision & Mission, http://www.mrcmekong.org/about-mrc/vision-and-mission (accessed 25 November 2015).

178 M. Osborne, *River at Risk: The Mekong and the Water Politics of China and Southeast Asia* (Double Bay: Longueville Media 2004), at 9.

179 A. Rieu-Clarke & G. Gooch, 'Governing the Tributaries of the Mekong—The Contribution of International Law and Institutions to Enhancing Equitable Cooperation Over the Sesan', 22 Pacific McGeorge Global Business and Development Law Journal (2009) 193–224, at 217.

180 Van Duyen, supra note 117, at 373.

research by the MRC Secretariat'[181] the results of which, 'confirm the immense value and productivity of the Mekong's capture fisheries, which are contingent on maintaining the ecological integrity of the Mekong river system.'[182]

Since its inception, the controversial issue of hydropower dams, especially those on the mainstream of the Mekong River, but also on certain tributaries, has been at the centre of much of the MRC's work.[183] In this regard, the MRC has performed a variety of facilitative and policy-making functions within the limits of its mandate in order to inform and try to improve the impact analysis, negotiation and decision-making processes, as well as to provide the tools and knowledge base for its member states on large-scale hydropower projects.[184]

The final key area of the Mekong Agreement related to the settlement of disputes. Pursuant to the Agreement, parties should first seek to resolve any 'difference or dispute'[185] through the Joint Committee and Council. Failing that, the Agreement provides that, 'the issue shall be referred to the governments to take cognizance of the matter for resolution by negotiation through diplomatic channels within a timely manner.'[186] Additionally, the parties are encouraged, 'should they find it necessary or beneficial', and by mutual agreement, to seek third-party support in order to resolve the dispute.[187]

181 G. Lee & N. Scurrah, *Power and Responsibility—The Mekong River Commission and Lower Mekong Mainstream Dams* (Sydney: Oxfam Australia & University of Sydney 2009), at 7.

182 Ibid.

183 See generally, F. Molle, T. Foran & M. Käkönen, *Contested Waterscapes in the Mekong Region—Hydropower, Livelihoods and Governance* (London: Earthscan 2010).

184 MRC, Basin Development Strategy 2016–2010, 5 April 2016, http://www.mrcmekong.org/assets/Publications/strategies-workprog/MRC-BDP-strategy-complete-final-02.16.pdf (accessed 25 November 2016); MRC, Guidelines for the Evaluation of Hydropower and Multi-purpose Project Portfolios, 2 November 2015 http://www.mrcmekong.org/assets/Publications/policies/1.-FINAL-ISH02-Guidelines-v1.5-updated-29Mar2016.pdf (accessed 25 November 2016); MRC, Guiding Considerations on Transboundary Monitoring for LMB Hydropower Planning and Management, 16 December 2014, http://www.mrcmekong.org/publications/topic/sustainable-hydropower, 25 November 2016; MRC, Rapid Basin-wide Hydropower Sustainability Assessment Tool, 2 December 2014, http://www.mrcmekong.org/assets/Publications/Reports/ISH-RST-Assessment-final-Draft-full-2013.pdf (accessed 25 November 2016).

185 While the terms 'difference' and 'dispute' are used within the Mekong Agreement, the distinction between them is not explained therein.

186 Art. 25, Mekong Agreement.

187 Art. 35, Mekong Agreement.

Between 2000 and 2008, the MRC codified a suite of procedures to complement the general provisions in the Mekong Agreement, namely: the Procedures for Data and Information Exchange and Sharing, approved in 2001;[188] Procedures for Water Use Monitoring, approved in 2003;[189] Procedures for Notification, Prior Consultation and Agreement (PNPCA), approved in 2003;[190] Procedures for Maintenance of Flows on the Mainstream, approved in 2006;[191] and Procedures for Water Quality, approved in 2011.[192] These Procedures have subsequently been accompanied by MRC Guidelines that are designed to assist in their implementation.[193] While these specific procedures were required to be developed under Articles 5, 6, and 26 of the Agreement, they are external to the treaty instrument and are not considered to be legally binding.[194]

---

188 MRC, Procedures for Data and Information Exchange, 1 November 2001, http://www.mrcmekong.org/assets/Publications/policies/Procedures-Data-Info-Exchange-n-Sharing.pdf (accessed 25 November 2016).

189 MRC, Procedures for Water Use Monitoring, 30 November 2003, http://www.mrcmekong.org/assets/Publications/policies/Procedures-Water-Use-Monitoring.pdf (accessed 25 November 2016).

190 MRC, Procedures for Notification, Prior Consultation and Agreement, 30 November 2003, http://www.mrcmekong.org/assets/Publications/policies/Procedures-Notification-Prior-Consultation-Agreement.pdf (accessed 25 November 2016) (PNPCA Procedures).

191 MRC, Procedures for the Maintenance of Flows on the Mainstream, 22 June 2006, http://www.mrcmekong.org/assets/Publications/policies/Procedures-Maintenance-Flows.pdf (accessed 25 November 2016).

192 MRC, Procedures for Water Quality, 26 January 2011, http://www.mrcmekong.org/assets/Publications/policies/Procedures-for-Water-Quality-council-approved260111.pdf (accessed 25 November 2016).

193 MRC, Guidelines on Implementation of the Procedures for Water Use Monitoring, 22 January 2006, http://www.mrcmekong.org/assets/Uploads/Tech-Guidelines-PWUM.pdf (accessed 25 November 2015); MRC, Guidelines on Implementation of the Procedures for Notification, Prior Consultation and Agreement, 31 August 2005, http://www.mrcmekong.org/publications/policies-procedures-and-guidelines/?start=10 (accessed 25 November 2016); MRC, Guidelines for Management of the Mekong River Commission Hydrometeorological Network, 31 August 2005, http://www.mrcmekong.org/assets/Uploads/Tech-Guidelines-Data-Info-Exchange-n-Sharing.pdf (accessed 25 November 2016).

194 Bearden et al., supra note 120, at 185; Q. Gao, *A Procedural Framework for Transboundary Water Management in the Mekong River Basin* (London: Brill 2014), at 152; B. Boer, et al., *The Mekong: A Socio-legal Approach to River Basin Development* (Abingdon: Routledge 2015), at 87; Y. Yasuda, *Rules, Norms and NGO Advocacy Strategies: Hydropower Development in the Mekong River* (Abingdon: Routledge 2015).

B Comparing the Mekong Agreement, the UN Watercourses Convention and the UNECE Water Convention

The previous section has provided an overview of the Mekong Agreement, the UN Watercourses Convention and the UNECE Water Convention. The purpose of this section is to investigate how the provisions from one or both global water conventions could translate to stronger principles and clarified processes for supporting transboundary river governance in the Mekong Basin. The similarities and differences between the two global water conventions and the Mekong Agreement will be considered. Ultimately, it is hoped that it will be possible to, firstly, ascertain if the two global water conventions are compatible with the Mekong Agreement; and secondly, whether there might be any gain for the states of the Mekong in joining one, or both, of the global water conventions in order to strengthen the Mekong Agreement.

I *Scope and Objectives*

The legal scope of an international watercourse agreement defines the functional reach of an agreement, the geographical and hydrological parameters to which it applies, and the subjects of the agreement.[195]

In terms of its functional scope, the Mekong Agreement might at first glance appear to adopt a broad approach in professing to cover, 'all fields of *sustainable* development, utilisation, management and conservation of the water and related resources of the Mekong *River Basin.*' [Emphasis added]. The UN Watercourses Convention and UNECE Water Convention might appear narrower in simply referring to the 'protection, preservation and management of international watercourses,'[196] and the 'protection and use of transboundary watercourses and international lakes,'[197] respectively. This raises the question of whether the concept of sustainability is adequately addressed in the two global water conventions, and also whether the use of the term 'river basin' in the Mekong Agreement offers a wider scope than the term 'watercourse', which is employed in both global water conventions.

Both of these issues will be addressed below. The geographical scope of the instruments will be examined, and secondly, the reach of the substantive

195 P.K. Wouters, et al., *Sharing Transboundary Waters—An Integrated Assessment of Equitable Entitlement* (Paris: UNESCO 2005), at 19; S. Vinogradov, P. Wouters & P. Jones, *Transforming Potential Conflict into Cooperation Potential: The Role of International Water Law* (Paris: UNESCO 2003), at 16.

196 Art. 1, UN Watercourses Convention.

197 Preamble, UNECE Water Convention.

and procedural norms will be considered. A further point to note concerning functional scope is that the Mekong Agreement professes to cover issues of navigation,[198] whereas the UN Watercourses Convention explicitly states that, '[t]he uses of international watercourses for navigation is not within the scope of the present Convention except insofar as other uses affect navigation or are affected by navigation.'[199] However, a review of all three instruments shows that there are no specific provisions dealing with the regulation of navigation.[200]

The geographical and hydrological terms and approaches adopted by the three instruments differ. The Mekong Agreement does not define the scope of the agreement, but adopts the term 'Mekong River Basin', and makes reference to the basin's 'water and related resources for navigational and non-navigational purposes.'[201] The agreement also uses the terms 'river basin', 'basin level', 'basin-wide', and 'river system' throughout the text, but without defining any of the terms.[202] Additionally, the Mekong Agreement refers to the term 'tributary' yet does not define it.[203] This distinction between the 'mainstream' and 'tributaries' within the text, without defining the difference, has significant legal ramifications for the prior notification and consultation procedures under the Agreement. This distinction will be discussed when comparing the procedural aspects of the legal instruments.

Rather than referring to the 'basin' or distinguishing between 'mainstream' and 'tributaries', both the UN Watercourses Convention and the UNECE Water Convention employ the more precise terms of 'international watercourse' and 'transboundary waters.' There is a difference between the definitions provided in the two global water instruments. The UNECE Water Convention stipulates

198 Article 1 of the Mekong Agreement sets out fields of cooperation, which include 'irrigation, hydro-power, navigation, flood control, fisheries, timber floating, recreation and tourism.'

199 Art. 1(2), UN Watercourses Convention.

200 In 1998, Vietnam and Cambodia entered into an Agreement on Waterway Transportation with the aim of reducing restrictions on cross-border navigation, and to improve efficiency and safety standards, see http://www.mrcmekong.org/assets/Publications/policies/agreement-waterway-trans-btw-Cam-n-VN-Eng.pdf (accessed 25 November 2016).

201 Preamble, Mekong Agreement.

202 For a commentary see, B.L. Bearden, 'Following the Proper Channels: Tributaries in the Mekong Legal Regime', 14(6) Water Policy (2012) 991–1014.

203 The term 'tributary' is defined in the PNPCA Procedures, supra note 190, which states that, '[f]or the purposes of the present Procedures, a tributary as decided by the JC [Joint Committee] is a natural stream of the Mekong River System whose flows have a significant impact on the mainstream. This definition is subject to be reviewed and agreed upon after some time of implementation if any concern is raised.'

that 'transboundary waters' refers to 'any surface or ground waters which mark, cross or are located on boundaries between two or more States,'[204] whereas the UN Watercourses Convention defines a 'watercourse' as, 'a system of surface waters and groundwaters constituting by virtue of their physical relationship a unitary whole.'[205] In the use of the phrase, 'surface or groundwaters', the UNECE Water Convention therefore adopts a wider approach than the UN Watercourses Convention by extending its scope beyond just groundwater connected to surface water to any groundwater that crosses sovereign boundaries.[206]

Whilst no explicit mention of groundwater is contained in the Mekong Agreement, it could be argued that the interconnectivity between surface water and groundwater is encompassed within the term 'basin.' Interpretative guidance on this point might be found in the 1966 International Law Association's (ILA) Helsinki Rules, which defines an 'international drainage basin' as 'a geographical area extending over two or more States determined by the watershed limits of the system of waters, including surface and underground waters, flowing into a common terminus.'[207] Several transboundary aquifers have been identified within the Mekong River Basin, namely the Lancang River Downstream Aquifer (China and Myanmar), the Mekong River midstream aquifer (Thailand, Laos and Vietnam), Khorat Plateau aquifer (Thailand and Laos), and the Mekong River delta aquifer (Cambodia and Vietnam).[208] In addition, groundwater overexploitation and pollution have been identified as major challenges faced by the states sharing these transboundary aquifers.[209] The need to recognise the linkages between groundwater and surface water within the Mekong Basin is evident.

In looking at approaches by which to strengthen cooperation over these transboundary aquifers, the Mekong states might turn to the 2008 ILC Draft Articles on Transboundary Aquifers[210] and the UNECE Model Provisions on

204 Art. 1(1).

205 Art. 2(1).

206 See UNECE, supra note 108, 21–16.

207 Art. II, Helsinki Rules, supra note 38.

208 K. Ha, et al., *Current Status and Issue of Groundwater in the Mekong River Basin* (Bangkok: KIGAM, CCOP & UNESCO 2015), at 50.

209 Ibid., at 53.

210 ILC, Draft Articles on Transboundary Aquifers, in UN General Assembly Official Records, 61st Session, Report of the International Law Commission, 2008, UN Doc. A/63/10; and UNECE, supra note 84. See also UN, 'While Management of Transboundary Aquifers Critical for 2030 Agenda Success, Draft Articles Must be Tailored to Each State, Speakers Tell Sixth Committee', 20 October 2016, UN Doc. GA/L/3528.

Transboundary Groundwaters.[211] As well as endorsing the key rules and principles that are found in the UN Watercourses Convention and the UNECE Water Convention, the UNECE Model Provisions and the ILC Draft Articles emphasise the need for states: to cooperate in the identification, delineation and characterisation of transboundary aquifers;[212] to jointly monitor the conditions of transboundary aquifers;[213] to develop joint management plans;[214] and to protect recharge and discharge zones of transboundary aquifers.[215] Both these latter instruments can therefore, to a large extent, be seen as complementing the more general rules and principles contained in the UN Watercourses Convention and the UNECE Water Convention, and could complement the existing 1995 Mekong Agreement with more bespoke provisions relating to transboundary aquifers.

In terms of the legal scope of the three instruments, some differences can be identified. The Mekong Agreement has, 'no retroactive effect upon activities and projects previously existing on the date of signature by the appointed plenipotentiaries.'[216] However, the Agreement does explicitly state that it replaces a number of existing agreements that relate to the Mekong River.[217] The Mekong Agreement goes on to stipulate that it does not, 'replace or take precedence over any other treaties, acts or agreements entered into by and among any of the parties hereto, except that where a conflict in terms, areas of jurisdiction of subject matter or operation of any entities created under existing agreements occurs with any provisions of this Agreement.'[218] This provision, while somewhat circular in nature, ultimately stipulates that the Mekong Agreement takes precedence over all matters covered thereunder. Such an approach might be contrasted by the UN Watercourses Convention, which stipulates that, 'nothing in the present Convention shall affect the rights or obligations of a watercourse State arising from agreements in force for it on the

211 https://www.unece.org/fileadmin/DAM/env/water/publications/WAT_model_provisions/ece_mp.wat_40_eng.pdf.

212 Provision 3, Model Provisions; and Art. 8, Draft Articles.

213 Provision 3, Model Provisions; and Art. 13, Draft Articles.

214 Provision 4 & 7, Model Provisions; and Art. 4, Draft Articles.

215 Provision 5(2), Model Provisions; and Art. 11, Draft Articles.

216 Art. 36, Mekong Agreement.

217 These are the Statute of the Committee for Coordination of Investigations of the Lower Mekong Basin of 1957 as amended, the Joint Declaration of Principles for Utilization of the Waters of the Lower Mekong Basin of 1975, the Declaration Concerning the Interim Committee for Coordination of Investigations of the Lower Mekong Basin of 1978, and all Rules of Procedures adopted under these agreements.

218 Art. 36(B), Mekong Agreement.

date on which it became a party to the present Convention.'[219] However, states are encouraged to consider harmonising existing agreements with the basic principles of the Convention.[220] The UNECE Water Convention is slightly more forceful on this point in that it requires its riparian parties to adapt existing agreements in order to ensure that they at least align to the basic principles set out in the Convention.[221] Whether or not the Mekong Agreement is consistent with the basic principles of the UNECE Water Convention will be explored in the subsequent sections.

Future agreements are also covered in both the UN Watercourses Convention and the UNECE Water Convention. Under the UN Watercourses Convention, there is no obligation to enter into watercourse agreements. Rather, the parties are encouraged to enter into agreements, 'which apply and adjust the provisions of the Convention to the characteristics and uses of a particular international watercourse or part thereof.'[222] This has implications that are directly relevant to the Mekong Basin in so far as under the UN Watercourses Convention, 'when some, but not all, watercourse states to a particular international watercourse are parties to an agreement, nothing in such an agreement would affect the rights or obligations under the Convention of watercourse states that are not parties to such an agreement.'[223]

The legal rights and duties of China and Myanmar as non-parties to the Mekong Agreement are therefore preserved if the current members of the Mekong Agreement all joined the Watercourses Convention. However, a slightly different approach is set forth under the UNECE Water Convention. Thereunder riparian parties must, 'enter into bilateral or multilateral agreements or other arrangements, where they do not exist' in order to support the implementation of the provisions of the Convention.[224] If China and Myanmar were also party to the UNECE Water Convention, they would, according to this latter requirement, be obliged to enter into an agreement with the other states of the Mekong River Basin. However, in the situation where the Lower Mekong Basin states were party to the UNECE Water Convention, and China and/or Myanmar were not members, then there would be no obligation on the lower

219 Art. 3(1), UN Watercourses Convention.

220 Art. 3(2), UN Watercourses Convention.

221 Art. 9, UNECE Watercourses Convention. See also supra note 89, and accompanying text.

222 Art. 3, UN Watercourses Convention.

223 S. Salman, 'Entry into Force of the UN Watercourses Convention: Why Should It Matter?', 31 International Journal of Water Resources Development (2014) 4–16, at. 8; See also Salman, supra note 29, at 5.

224 Art. 9(1), UNECE Water Convention.

Mekong states to enter agreements with these non-parties. Such a situation reflects a general obligation under customary international law, whereby states are obliged to negotiate agreements in good faith, but the law falls short of requiring those states to enter into an agreement.[225]

II *Substantive Norms*

(a) Equitable and Reasonable Utilisation

The Mekong Agreement, the UN Watercourses Convention and the UNECE Water Convention provide for similar substantive norms, although the norms are presented differently in each instrument.

Under the Mekong Agreement, states are obliged to, 'utilise the waters of the Mekong River System in a reasonable and equitable manner,' pursuant to relevant factors and circumstances.[226] However, the Agreement does not provide any list of relevant factors and circumstances. In determining what is equitable and reasonable, some guidance is provided through the requirement that the parties cooperate in the maintenance of flows on the mainstream in order to: provide an acceptable minimum monthly natural flow during each month of the dry season; enable an acceptable natural reverse flow of the Tonlé Sap during the wet season; and prevent average daily peak flows that are greater than those that naturally occur during the flood season.[227] Furthermore, the Mekong Agreement commits the parties to develop Rules for Water Utilisation and Inter-Basin Diversions, which should establish a timeframe for the wet and dry seasons; set the location of hydrological stations, and determine and maintain flow level requirements for each station; and set criteria for determining surplus quantities of water during the dry season on the mainstream.[228] However, to date, the Rules for Water Utilisation and Inter-Basin Diversions have not been fully completed.

Both the UN Watercourses Convention and UNECE Water Convention also oblige states to utilise their international watercourses in an equitable and reasonable manner.[229] However, the UN Watercourses Convention goes further by listing the factors and circumstances that should be taken into account in determining what is equitable and reasonable. Article 6 of the latter instrument sets out those factors and circumstances as including: the natural characteristics of an international watercourse; the socio-economic needs of the

225 See Lake Lannoux Arbitration (France v. Spain), 24 ILR (1957) 101.

226 Art. 5, Mekong Agreement.

227 Art. 6, Mekong Agreement.

228 Art. 26, Mekong Agreement.

229 Art. 5, UN Watercourses Convention and Art. 2(C), UNECE Water Convention.

watercourse states concerned; the population dependent on the watercourse in each watercourse state; the effects of the use or uses of the watercourses in one watercourse state on other watercourse states; existing and potential uses of the watercourse; conservation, protection, development and economy of use of the water resources of the watercourse and the costs of measures taken to that effect; and the availability of alternatives to a particular existing or planned use.[230] The UN Watercourses Convention goes on to stipulate that in determining what is equitable and reasonable, special regard must be given to the requirements of 'vital human needs.'[231] 'Vital human needs' encompass, 'sufficient water to sustain human life, including both drinking water and water required for the production of food in order to prevent starvation.'[232] Within the context of the Mekong, water to sustain livelihoods from fisheries and agriculture might be seen as falling within the category of vital human needs. It could therefore be argued that the UN Watercourses Convention helps support the interpretation of the more general provisions found in the Mekong Agreement when interpreting the principle of equitable and reasonable utilisation, and places particular emphasis on the need to protect vital human needs.

(b) Duty to Take All Appropriate Measures to Prevent Significant Harm

The duty to take all appropriate measures to prevent significant harm is covered in the Mekong Agreement, the UN Watercourses Convention and the UNECE Water Convention. However, each instrument includes different terminology and formulations, which raises a question over their compatibility.

As noted previously, under the Mekong Agreement, states are under a general obligation to, 'make every effort to *avoid, minimise and mitigate* harmful effects that might occur to the environment [emphasis added],'[233] This requirement has some similarity with the UNECE Water Convention, which requires parties to, 'take all appropriate measures to *prevent, control and*

---

230 Art. 6, UN Watercourses Convention.

231 Art. 10, UN Watercourses Convention.

232 Draft Articles on the Law of the Non-navigational Uses of International Watercourses and Commentaries Thereto in *Yearbook of the International Law Commission*, 1994, Vol. II (pt. 2) (1994 Draft Articles), at 110. See, P.H. Gleick, 'The Human Right to Water', 1 Water Policy (1998) 487–503, at 495; H. Shuval, 'Meeting Vital Human Needs: Equitable Resolution of Conflicts Over Shared Water Resources of Israelis and Palestinians', in H. Shuval & H. Dweik, *Water Resources in the Middle East* (Berlin: Springer 2007), 3–16; S. McCaffrey, supra note 9, at 255.

233 Art. 7, Mekong Agreement.

reduce any transboundary impact [emphasis added]', and the duty under the UN Watercourses Convention to 'take all appropriate measures to *prevent* the causing of significant harm [emphasis added].'[234]

However, a number of differences between the three instruments can be seen in the formulation of this obligation to prevent significant harm.

Firstly, the object of the duty differs slightly. The UN Watercourses Convention refers to, 'significant harm to other watercourse States.'[235] The ILC has suggested that 'The term "significant" is not without ambiguity and a determination has to be made in each specific case.'[236] However, it goes on to suggest that, 'significant', 'is something more than "detectable" but need not be at the level of "serious" or "substantial." The harm must lead to a real detrimental effect on matters such as, for example, human health, industry, property, environment or agriculture in other States.'[237]

In contrast, the UNECE Water Convention incorporates a threshold into the definition of 'transboundary impact', namely, 'any *significant adverse effect* on the environment resulting from a change in the conditions of transboundary waters caused by a human activity, the physical origin of which is situated wholly or in part within an area under the jurisdiction of a Party, within an area under the jurisdiction of another Party [emphasis added].'[238]

In the opinion of the ILC, the term 'significant adverse effect' is considered to be a lower threshold than that of 'significant harm.'[239] Both formulations differ from the Mekong Agreement, which in the first part of Article 7 simply refers to 'harmful effects that might occur to the environment.'[240] However, all three instruments qualify this so-called 'no harm' obligation. In the Mekong Agreement, states are under an obligation to '*make every effort* to avoid, minimize and mitigate harmful effects that might occur to the environment.'[241] Under the UNECE Water Convention and the UN Watercourses Convention, the states are obliged to take 'all appropriate measures' to 'prevent the causing significant harm to other watercourse States' (in the case of the UN Watercourses Convention), and 'prevent, control and reduce any transboundary impact'

234 Art. 1(1), UNECE Water Convention.
235 Art. 7, UN Watercourses Convention.
236 Draft Articles on Prevention of Transboundary Harm from Hazardous Activities, with Commentaries, in *Yearbook of the International*, 2001, Vol. II (pt. 2), at 152.
237 Ibid.
238 Art. 1, UNECE Water Convention.
239 1994 Draft Articles, supra note 232, at 111.
240 Art. 7, Mekong Agreement.
241 Art. 7, Mekong Agreement.

(in the case of the UNECE Water Convention). The ILC has described this obligation as one of 'due diligence', and further commented that, '[i]t is not intended to guarantee that in utilizing an international watercourse significant harm would not occur. It is an obligation of conduct, and an obligation of result.'[242] The precise application of this obligation will depend both on the nature of the activity in question and the capacity of states to prevent, control or reduce such harm. States with greater capacity (technical or financial) to prevent harm may be placed under a higher standard that other states. Similarly, where there is a risk that an activity may cause irreparable harm to the environment, more stringent measure to prevention such harm will be required; whereas in other circumstances it might suffice that a state minimizes or controls the harm in question.

This due diligence standard, which is provided for in each of the legal instruments, leaves the states with considerable discretion to determine, firstly, what measures might be put in place, and secondly, whether harm should be prevented, controlled or reduced. The ILC has suggested that this so-called 'duty of conduct' is one that would require a state to enforce its laws, prevent or terminate illegal activity, or punish those that might be responsible for breaching those laws.[243] The ICJ has also suggested that an Environmental Impact Assessment (EIA) can be considered to be part of a due diligence obligation where there is a risk of transboundary harm.[244] The UN Watercourses Convention also suggests that appropriate measures to prevent, reduce and control pollution might include: setting joint water quality objectives and criteria; establishing techniques and practices to address pollution from point and non-point sources; and establishing lists of substances whose introduction into the waters of an international watercourse would be prohibited, limited, investigated or monitored.'[245] Additional 'appropriate' measures might be interpreted from the procedural requirements contained in the UN Watercourses Convention and UNECE Water Convention (as discussed below).

However, in the context of transboundary waters, the UNECE Water Convention provides the most detail related to 'appropriate measures.' In Article 3, the UNECE Water Convention stipulates that, in order to:

242 1994 Draft Articles, supra note 232, at 103. See also J. Kulesza, *Due Diligence in International Law* (London: Brill 2016); R.P. Barnidge, 'The Due Diligence Principle under International Law', 8(1) International Community Law Review (2006) 81–121.

243 1994 Draft Articles, supra note 232, at 103.

244 ICJ, Case Concerning Pulp Mills on the River Uruguay (Argentina v. Uruguay), Judgement, 20 April 2010, para. 204.

245 Art. 21(3), UN Watercourses Convention.

prevent, control and reduce transboundary impact, the parties shall develop, adopt, implement and, as far as possible, render compatible relevant legal, administrative, economic, financial and technical measures, in order to ensure, *inter alia*, that:

(a) The emission of pollutants is prevented, controlled and reduced at source through the application of, *inter alia*, low- and non-waste technology;
(b) Transboundary waters are protected against pollution from point sources through the prior licensing of waste-water discharges by the competent national authorities, and that the authorized discharges are monitored and controlled;
(c) Limits for waste-water discharges stated in permits are based on the best available technology for discharges of hazardous substances;
(d) Stricter requirements, even leading to prohibition in individual cases, are imposed when the quality of the receiving water or the ecosystem so requires;
(e) At least biological treatment or equivalent processes are applied to municipal waste-water, where necessary in a step-by-step approach;
(f) Appropriate measures are taken, such as the application of the best available technology, in order to reduce nutrient inputs from industrial and municipal sources;
(g) Appropriate measures and best environmental practices are developed and implemented for the reduction of inputs of nutrients and hazardous substances from diffuse sources, especially where the main sources are from agriculture (guidelines for developing best environmental practices are given in annex II to this Convention);
(h) Environmental impact assessment and other means of assessment are applied;
(i) Sustainable water-resources management, including the application of the ecosystems approach, is promoted;
(j) Contingency planning is developed;
(k) Additional specific measures are taken to prevent the pollution of groundwaters; and
(l) The risk of accidental pollution is minimized.[246]

246 Art. 3, UNECE Water Convention.

In setting out the key measures that states should adopt in order to prevent, control and reduce transboundary impact, the UNECE Water Convention offers additional interpretative guidance to the more general 'make every effort' requirement under the UN Watercourses Convention.

Another area in which the UNECE Water Convention adds further interpretive guidance relates to the definition of 'harm' or 'impact.' 'Harm' is not defined in the UN Watercourses Convention. Under the Mekong Agreement, 'harmful effects' are described as including, 'the water quantity and quality, the aquatic (eco-system) conditions, and ecological balance of the river system, from the development and use of the Mekong River Basin water resources or discharge of wastes and return flows.'[247] The UNECE Water Convention goes further by providing the most detailed account of 'transboundary impact', which includes, 'effects on human health and safety, flora, fauna, soil, air, water, climate, landscape and historical monuments or other physical structures or the interaction among these factors; they also include effects on the cultural heritage or socio-economic conditions resulting from alterations to those factors.'[248]

(c) The Relationship between Equitable and Reasonable Utilisation and No Significant Harm

The two global water conventions clearly set out the relationship between the principle of equitable and reasonable utilisation, and the duty to prevent significant harm.[249] The UN Watercourses Convention provides that where significant harm occurs, the states must consider whether or not it might be eliminated or mitigated on the basis of equity.[250] The primacy of the principle of equitable and reasonable utilisation is therefore secured pursuant to the UN Watercourses Convention. The UNECE Water Convention obliges its parties to, 'take all appropriate measures', 'to ensure that transboundary waters are used in a reasonable and equitable way.'[251] The principle of equitable and reasonable utilisation under the UNECE Water Convention would therefore

---

247 Art. 7, Mekong Agreement.

248 Art. 1(2), UNECE Water Convention.

249 See A.E. Utton, 'Which Rule Should Prevail in International Water Disputes: That of Reasonableness or That of No Harm', 36 Natural Resources Journal (1996) 635–641; P. Wouters, 'An Assessment of Recent Developments in International Watercourse Law Through the Prism of the Substantive Rules Governing Use Allocation', 36(2) Natural Resources Journal (1996) 417–439.

250 Art. 7(2), UN Watercourses Convention.

251 Art. 2(1), UNECE Water Convention.

dictate what measures are deemed appropriate in the prevention, control or reduction of transboundary impact.

While the two global instruments therefore seek to reach the same goal, and use equitable and reasonable utilisation as the guiding principle, the Mekong Agreement is less clear on this matter. Article 7 provides a general obligation upon parties to 'make every effort to avoid, minimise and mitigate harmful effects that might occur to the environment.' As noted above, while this might be seen as a due diligence obligation, it does not state whether such harm must be transboundary, nor does it state how it relates to the obligation under Article 5 of the Mekong Agreement, 'to utilise the waters of the Mekong River system in a reasonable and equitable manner.' Article 7 does go on to stipulate that, '[w]here one or more State is notified with proper and valid evidence that it is causing substantial damage to one or more riparians from the use of and/or discharge to water of the Mekong River, that state or states shall cease immediately the alleged cause of harm until such harm is determined in accordance with Article 8.'

Article 8 goes on to provide that:

> Where harmful effects cause substantial damage to one or more riparians from the use of and/or discharge to waters of the Mekong River by any riparian state, the party(ies) concerned shall determine all relevant factors, the cause, extent of damage and responsibility for damages caused by that State in conformity with principles of international law relating to state responsibility.[252]

Under Articles 7 and 8 there is no reference to the principle of equitable and reasonable utilisation. It is therefore unclear how these provisions relate to the previous requirements, both in Article 7 itself, 'to make every effort to avoid, minimise and mitigate harmful effects that might occur to the environment', and the obligation in Article 5 to utilise the waters of the Mekong River system in an equitable and reasonable manner. In sum, the UN Watercourses Convention and the UNECE Water Convention could assist in the interpretation of the Mekong Agreement by clearly stipulating the relationship between the principles of equitable and reasonable utilisation, and no significant harm.

---

252 The ILC considered the threshold of 'substantial' to be higher than that of 'significant.' The ILC commented that, '[w]hile such an effect must be capable of being established by objective evidence and not be trivial in nature, it need not rise to the level of being substantial', at 94.

(d) The Protection of Ecosystems

A further feature of the UN Watercourses Convention, the UNECE Water Convention and the Mekong Agreement relates to ecosystem protection and sustainable development.

The Mekong Agreement recognises the importance of developing the basin in a sustainable manner multiple times—in its title, preamble and objectives. The agreement also stipulates that the parties must, 'protect the environment, natural resources, aquatic life and conditions, and ecological balance of the Mekong River Basin from pollution or other harmful effects resulting from any development plans and uses of water and related resources in the Basin.'[253] Moreover, states are obliged to maintain flows of the mainstream of the Mekong River Basin—although the extent to which such flows are to satisfy ecosystem needs is not clearly stated.

The UN Watercourses Convention places significant emphasis on the need to develop international watercourses in a sustainable manner. Article 5(1) stipulates that states should, when determining what is equitable and reasonable, aim towards, 'attaining optimal and sustainable utilisation thereof, and benefits therefrom' an international watercourse, 'consistent with adequate protection of the watercourse.' The need to protect the watercourse is stressed again in Article 5(2), which obliges states to, 'participate in the ... protection of an international watercourse in an equitable and reasonable manner.'[254] Furthermore, Article 20 of the UN Watercourses Convention obliges watercourse states to, 'protect and preserve the ecosystems of international watercourses.'[255]

The UNECE Water Convention obliges states to take all appropriate measures, 'to ensure that transboundary waters are used with the aim of ecologically

253 Art. 3, Mekong Agreement.

254 Art. 6 stipulates that the parties agree:

"To cooperate in the maintenance of the flows on the mainstream from diversions, storage releases, or other actions of a permanent nature; except in the cases of historically severe droughts and/or floods:

A. Of not less than the acceptable minimum monthly natural flow during each month of the dry season;

B. To enable the acceptable natural reverse flow of the Tonle Sap to take place during the wet season; and,

C. To prevent average daily peak flows greater than what naturally occur on the average during the flood season."

255 See also Art. 21 on prevention, reduction and control of pollution; Art. 22 on the introduction of alien or new species; and Art. 23 on protection and preservation of the marine environment.

sound and rational water management, conservation of water resources and environmental protection'; and 'to ensure conservation and, where necessary, restoration of ecosystems.'[256] In addition, the UNECE Water Convention requires states to take into account the precautionary principle, the polluter-pays principle, and intergenerational equity, in determining taking appropriate measure to prevent, control and reduce transboundary impact.[257]

In placing particular emphasis on the need to protect the environment or ecosystem of an international watercourse, each of the three instruments might therefore be seen as complementary. Moreover, a combined reading of their text might help strengthen the extent to which ecosystems needs and interests are weighed up against each other when applying the principle of equitable and reasonable utilisation.

III *Procedural Aspects*

Procedural mechanisms are critical to the implementation of the substantive norms that are contained within the Mekong Agreement, the UN Watercourses Convention and the UNECE Water Convention.[258]

These procedural requirements are founded upon a general obligation to cooperate, which is expressed in the Mekong Agreement, the UN Watercourses Convention and the UNECE Water Convention.[259] The three instruments also contain more specific procedural requirements relating to notification and consultation and data and information exchange.

The Mekong Agreement, the UN Watercourses Convention and the UNECE Water Convention all place states under an obligation to notify and consult with each other concerning planned measures. However, there are notable differences between the three instruments. In terms of who to notify, the UN Watercourses Convention limits this to other watercourse states that may suffer a significant adverse effect from a planned measure.[260] Conversely, the Mekong Agreement simply requires notification to take place via the Joint Committee, which includes representatives from the four lower Mekong states.[261] Similarly, the UNECE Water Convention obliges states to establish

---

256 Art. 2(2)(B) & (D), UNECE Water Convention.

257 Art. (2)(5).

258 McIntyre, supra note 53.

259 Art. 4, Mekong Agreement, Art. 8, UN Watercourses Convention, and Art. 9, UNECE Water Convention. See also C. Leb, *Cooperation in the Law of Transboundary Water Resources* (Cambridge: Cambridge University Press 2013).

260 Art. 12, UN Watercourses Convention.

261 Chapter II, Mekong Agreement.

joint bodies, which *inter alia*, 'serve as a forum for the exchange of information on existing and planned uses of water and related institutions that are likely to cause transboundary impact.'[262]

The timing of notification is addressed both in the UN Watercourses Convention and the Mekong Agreement, with both instruments requiring that such notification be 'timely.'[263] Any notification should also be accompanied with sufficient data and information in order for other states to evaluate the potential effect of the measure.

The UN Watercourses Convention requires the planning state to share, 'available technical data and information, including the results of any environmental impact assessment.'[264] A similar requirement is contained in the Mekong Agreement, which in the case of prior consultation, requires states to provide, 'data and information ... that would allow the other member riparians to discuss and evaluate the impact of the proposed use upon their uses of water and any other affects.'[265] While the UNECE Water Convention does not explicitly cover the type of data and information that a notifying state should exchange, it does stipulate that any joint bodies established by the parties should, 'participate in the implementation of environmental impact assessments relating to transboundary waters, in accordance with appropriate international regulations.'[266]

Having notified and exchanged relevant data and information, the UN Watercourses Convention then provides a period of six months for potentially affected states to respond to the notifying state.[267] Pursuant to the Convention,

262 Art. 9(2)(h), UNECE Water Convention. For UNECE States, the UNECE Water Convention is also complemented by the Convention on Environmental Impact Assessment within a Transboundary Context (1991) (Espoo Convention). The ESPOO Convention sets out detailed requirements by which states must notify and consult on planned measures, and also contact transboundary Environmental Impact Assessments.

263 Art. 12, UN Watercourses Convention; Chapter II, Mekong Agreement.

264 Art. 12, UN Watercourses Convention. This requirement to provide an Environmental Impact Assessment 'if available' could be interpreted two ways. Firstly, it might suggest that it is at the discretion of the notifying state whether or not to provide an environmental impact assessment. Secondly, and more likely in light of subsequent developments in customary international law, it can be argued that an environmental impact assessment, which considers the transboundary aspects of any development, is a due diligence obligation upon all states (see supra note 264). However, as noted in the Pulp Mills Case (supra note 62), notification may well precede the environmental impact assessment process.

265 Chapter II, Mekong Agreement.

266 Art. 9(2)(J), UNECE Water Convention.

267 Art. 13(a), UN Watercourses Convention.

this period may be extended by a further six months if a notified state has 'special difficulty' in evaluating the project within the initial six months.[268] During the six- or 12-month period, the notifying state is obliged not to, 'implement or permit the implementation of the planned measures without the consent of the notified State.'[269] If the states in question fail to agree on the best way forward during the notification period, they are required under the UN Watercourses Convention to enter into consultations and negotiations with a view to reaching an equitable resolution of the situation.[270] During the negotiation and consultation period, the notifying state must, unless agreed otherwise, refrain from implementing the planned measure for a period of six months.[271]

Within the Mekong context, an attempt to provide additional guidance related to notification and consultation resulted in the adoption of the PNPCA, which were signed by the MRC Council members in 2003.[272] The PNPCA were complemented by Guidelines on Implementation of the PNPCA Guidelines, which were signed by members of the MRC Joint Committee.[273] The PNPCA provide both the content and form that notification and prior consultation should take; that the consultation period should be six months and extended if necessary; and the procedures also set out the roles and responsibilities of the MRC National Mekong Committees, Joint Committee and Secretariat throughout the process.[274] For both notification and prior consultation, prescribed forms are set out in the annex of the PNPCA. These forms require the states planning a project to provide: the name of the project, location and nature of the proposed project; the purpose of the proposed use; expected dates for construction and starting operation; and key documents, including a summary of a feasibility study and an initial environmental evaluation.[275] The PNPCA Guidelines go further in a number of key areas, including the timing of notification, roles and responsibilities and the data and information that should be shared. However, while the PNPCA and PNPCA Guidelines are largely consistent with the UN Watercourses Convention, it is questionable as to whether they are legally

268 Art. 13(b), UN Watercourses Convention.

269 Art. 13(b), UN Watercourses Convention.

270 Art. 17, UN Watercourses Convention.

271 Art. 17(3), UN Watercourses Convention.

272 PNPCA Procedures supra note 190.

273 Supra note 193.

274 PNPCA Procedures supra note 190.

275 Ibid.

binding.[276] Moreover, the UN Watercourses Convention provides additional details on what happens if the states fail to agree following the consultation process. Notification and consultation procedures is therefore an area where the Mekong Agreement might benefit from the more detailed and legally binding requirements of the UN Watercourses Convention.[277]

Closely aligned to the requirement to notify and consult is the more general requirement that states exchange data and information relating to their international watercourses. Both global water conventions place states under an obligation to exchange such data and information. The UN Watercourses Convention requires parties to exchange, 'on a regular basis, data and information concerning, 'the condition of the watercourse, in particular that of a hydrological, meteorological, hydrogeological and ecological nature and related to the water quality as well as related forecasts.'[278] Watercourse states are also compelled, upon a request from another state, to share data and information that is not readily available. In such circumstances, data and information might be shared on the condition that the requesting state covers reasonable costs associated with gathering the data and information.[279] However, data and information that is vital to a state's 'national defence or security' can be excluded from this general obligation to exchange data and information.[280]

The UNECE Water Convention provides a general requirement that parties, 'provide for the widest exchange of information', and to do so, 'as early as possible.'[281] More specific requirements are placed on riparian parties, who are obligated to exchange data and information on matters including: the environmental conditions of transboundary waters; experience gained in the application and operation of best available technology and results of research and development; emission and monitoring data; measures taken and planned to be taken to prevent, control and reduce transboundary impact; national

276 Supra note 194.

277 R. Kinna, 'UN Watercourses Convention: Can It Revitalise the Mekong Agreement 20 Years On?' Mekong Commons, 24 November 2015, http://www.mekongcommons.org/un-watercourses-convention-can-it-revitalise-mekong-agreement-20-years-on (accessed 5 December 2016); R. Kinna, R., 'An Alternate Past/Future for Mekong River Dams under the UN Watercourses Convention (Parts 1, 2 and 3), Global Water Forum, 4 April 2016, Global Water Forum, http://www.globalwaterforum.org/2016/04/04/an-alternate-past-future-for-mekong-river-dams-under-the-un-watercourses-convention-part-1 (accessed 5 December 2016).

278 Art. 9, UN Watercourses Convention.

279 Art. 9(2), UN Watercourses Convention.

280 Art. 31, UN Watercourses Convention.

281 Art. 6, UNECE Water Convention.

regulations relating to emission limits; and permits or regulations for wastewater discharges issued by a competent authority or appropriate body.[282] Along similar lines to the UN Watercourses Convention, the UNECE Water Convention provides that a riparian party may request another riparian party to provide data and information that is not available; and such a request may be conditioned that the requesting party pay reasonable costs for security of that data or information.[283] However, the UNECE Water Convention and the UN Watercourses Convention do differ slightly in the type of data and information that might be protected. As well as protecting data and information related to 'national security', the UNECE Water Convention also protects data and information, 'related to industrial and commercial secrecy, including intellectual security.'[284] This condition is slightly tempered by the requirement in the UNECE Water Convention that riparian parties, 'facilitate the exchange of best available technology, particularly through the promotion of the commercial exchange of available technology; direct industrial contacts and cooperation, including joint ventures; the exchange of information and experience; and the provision of technical assistance.[285]

The Mekong Agreement does not dedicate a specific provision to data and information exchange. However, a task of the Joint Committee is, '[t]o regularly obtain, update and exchange information and data necessary' to the implement the Agreement. Additionally, Procedures for Data and Information Exchange and Sharing were signed by the members of the MRC Council on 1st of November 2001.[286] The procedures provide that the data and information to be shared between the parties should include that relating to water resources, topography, natural resources, agriculture, navigation and transport, flood management and mitigation, infrastructure, urbanisation or industrialisation, environment or ecology, administrative boundaries, socio-economy, and tourism.[287] In line with the UNECE Water Convention, both data and information relating to national defence or security, and that of a commercially sensitive nature, is exempt from the general principle of data and information

282 Art. 13(1), UNECE Water Convention.

283 Art. 13(3), UNECE Watercourses Convention.

284 Art. 8, UNECE Water Convention.

285 Art. 13(4), UNECE Water Convention.

286 Supra note 188.

287 Section 4, supra note 188.

exchange.[288] The procedures also provide that costs for collecting data and information should be borne by the requesting party.[289]

As with the PNPCA and their Guidelines, the Procedures on data and information exchange and sharing go some way to address the gaps in the Mekong Agreement related to data and information, although the question over the legal status still remains.[290] The UN Watercourses Convention and the UNECE Water Convention, if the Mekong states were to become party, would therefore strengthen the requirement for data and information exchange.

The UN Watercourses Convention and the UNECE Water Convention contain a number of additional procedural mechanisms that might strengthen the implementation of the Mekong Agreement.

The UNECE Water Convention requires riparian parties to, 'implement joint programmes for monitoring the conditions of transboundary waters, including floods and ice drifts, as well as transboundary impact.'[291] In so doing, parties are obliged to agree upon pollution parameters and pollutants, which must be regularly monitored.[292] Riparian parties are also obliged to conduct 'joint or coordinated assessments of the conditions of transboundary waters and the effectiveness of measures taken for the prevention, control and reduction of transboundary impact.'[293] A further requirement under the UNECE Water Convention is that riparian parties, 'harmonise rules for the setting up and operation of monitoring programmes, measurement systems, devices, analytical techniques, data processing and evaluation procedures, and methods for the registration of pollutants discharged.'[294]

As well as requirements related to monitoring and assessment, the UNECE Water Convention obliges riparian states to make publicly available, 'information on the conditions of transboundary waters, measures taken or planned to be taken to prevent, control and reduce transboundary impact, and the effectiveness of those measures.'[295] While the UNECE Water Convention does not contain a similar provision, it does refer to a right of 'persons, natural or juridical' to seek access to justice in a foreign court if they have, 'suffered or are

288 Section 4, supra note 188.

289 Section 4, supra note 188.

290 Supra note 194.

291 Art. 11(1), UNECE Water Convention. See also Article 4, which stipulates that, '[t]he Parties shall establish programmes for monitoring the conditions of transboundary waters.'

292 Article 11(2), UNECE Water Convention.

293 Art. 11(3), UNECE Water Convention.

294 Art. 11(4), UNECE Water Convention.

295 Art. 16, UNECE Water Convention.

under a serious threat of suffering significant transboundary harm as a result of activities related to an international watercourse.' The Mekong Agreement does not contain any provision relating to non-state activities.

An additional area that is covered by the UN Watercourses Convention and the UNECE Water Convention but not the Mekong Agreement concerns emergency situations. Pursuant to the UN Watercourses Convention, such situations include, 'a situation that causes, or poses an imminent threat of causing, serious harm to watercourse states or other states and that results suddenly from natural causes, such as floods, the breaking up of ice, landslides or earthquakes, or from human conduct, such as industrial accidents.'[296] Both the UN Watercourse Convention and the UNECE Water Convention require that states, 'without delay and by the most expeditious means available', notify potentially affected states or competent international organisations of any emergency situations arising in their territory.[297] The UN Watercourses Convention also requires states to develop contingency plans for responding to such emergencies,[298] and the UNECE Water Convention requires that the parties, 'operate coordinated or joint communication, warning and alarm systems with the aim of obtaining and transmitting information.'[299]

IV *Institutional Arrangements*

The institutional arrangements envisaged by the UN Watercourses Convention, the UNECE Water Convention and the Mekong Agreement differ between each legal instrument.

The UN Watercourses Convention simply provides a general recommendation that states 'enter into consultation', with a view to the establishment of 'joint management mechanisms.'[300]

The UNECE Water Convention goes further by requiring that riparian parties establish 'joint bodies' related to their transboundary waters.[301] While there is flexibility in the form that such 'joint bodies' might take,[302] the UNECE Water Convention does set out a number of tasks that such bodies must perform, including: collecting, compiling and evaluating data in order to identify

296 Art. 28, UN Watercourses Convention.

297 Art. 28(2), UN Watercourses Convention, and Art. 14, UNECE Water Convention.

298 Art. 28(4), UN Watercourses Convention.

299 Art. 14, UNECE Water Convention. See also Art. 15 relating to mutual assistance regarding emergency situations.

300 Supra note 67.

301 Art. 9(2), UNECE Water Convention.

302 Guide to Implementing the UNECE Water Convention, supra note 62, at 70–76.

pollution sources likely to cause transboundary impact; elaborating joint monitoring programmes concerning water quality and quantity; drawing up inventories and exchanging information on the pollution sources; elaborating emission limits for waste water and evaluating the effectiveness of control programmes; elaborating joint water-quality objectives and criteria, and proposing relevant measures for maintaining, and where necessary, improving water quality; developing concerted action programmes for the reduction of pollution loads from point and diffuse sources; establishing early warning and alarm procedures; serving as a forum for exchanging information on existing and planned uses; promoting cooperation and exchange of information on the best available technology; and participating in the implementation of environmental impact assessments.[303]

As noted previously, the Mekong Agreement sets out the international framework for its implementation, namely the MRC. The MRC would fall under the meaning of a 'joint body', as envisaged in the UNECE Water Convention. A number of tasks of the MRC are also set out in the Agreement. The functions of the MRC Council are described in broad terms, including making policies and decisions in support of implementing the Mekong Agreement, as well as approving rules of water utilisation, creating a basin development plan and establishing guidelines for financial and technical assistance for development projects and programmes.[304] More specific functions are set out for the MRC Joint Committee, which include: implementing the policies and decisions of the MRC Council; formulating a basin development plan and obtaining financial support for it; regularly obtaining, updating and exchanging information and data to support the implementation of the Agreement; conducting 'appropriate studies and assessments' for protecting the ecological balance of the Mekong River Basin; assigning and supervising tasks of the Secretariat; seeking to address and resolve any differences between the parties; reviewing and approving studies and training for personnel of each riparian party; and making recommendations to the Council on the organisational structure of the Secretariat.[305] The Secretariat itself is afforded the following functions under the Agreement: carrying out decision and tasks assigned by the Council and Joint Committee; providing technical and financial administration and advice to the Council and Joint Committee; formulating a work programme and other plans, projects, programme documents, studies and assessments as required; assisting the Joint Committee in the implementation and management of

303 Art. 9(2)(a)–(j), UNECE Water Convention.

304 Art. 18, Mekong Agreement.

305 Art. 24, Mekong Agreement.

projects and programmes; maintaining a database of information; and making preparations for sessions of the Council and Joint Committee.[306]

Comparing the task of joint bodies under the UNECE Water Convention and the functions of the MRC shows some differences. The functions of the MRC Council, Joint Committee and Secretariat are, pursuant to the Mekong Agreement, more general in nature. Conversely, the UNECE Water Convention envisaged a number of more specific tasks that joint bodies must perform, including supporting environmental impact assessment processing, developing concerted action programmes on pollution prevention, setting joint water-quality objectives and criteria, and establishing joint monitoring programmes. In practice, a number of these tasks have been conducted by the MRC. A question could therefore be raised over whether including more specific and legally binding commitments related to the tasks of the MRC would be advantageous.

V *Dispute Settlement*

The final area of comparison between the three legal instruments relates to dispute settlement mechanisms. Again, there are considerable differences between each instrument.

The UN Watercourses Convention has the most detailed provision relating to dispute settlement. In the event of a dispute, the parties in question shall first seek to settle their dispute by negotiation, good offices, mediation and conciliation through a joint watercourse institution, arbitration or the ICJ.[307] If, after six months, the dispute remains unresolved, then one or both parties can submit the dispute to an impartial third-party 'fact-finding commission.'[308] The fact-finding commission is charged with investigating the facts of the dispute and coming up with a recommendation on how the dispute might be resolved in an equitable manner.[309] States are obliged to consider the recommendation of the third-party fact-finding commission in good faith but are not obligated to implement it.[310] That the UN Watercourses Convention obliges parties to a dispute to submit to an independent fact-finding commission is crucial to its objective of resolution, as it effectively takes the facts of the dispute out of the vested interests of those states involved and places them in an *open and transparent* sphere for independent investigation, evaluation and finally, recommendations. As noted earlier, in the absence of meaningful

306 Art. 30, Mekong Agreement.
307 Art. 33(2), UN Watercourses Convention.
308 Art. 33(3), UN Watercourses Convention.
309 Art. 33(8), UN Watercourses Convention.
310 Art. 33(8), UN Watercourses Convention.

cooperation and good faith between the disputing states, ultimately the direct involvement of an independent third party in dispute settlement on a case-by-case basis may be critical to the resolution of any watercourse dispute.[311]

The UNECE Water Convention provides a more general requirement that parties settle their disputes, 'by negotiation or by any other means of dispute settlement acceptable to the parties of the dispute.'[312] When becoming party to the Convention, or at any time thereafter, states may also declare that if disputes are not resolved through negotiation or other means, the dispute will be submitted to the ICJ or arbitration.[313] Under the UNECE Water Convention, the parties have established the Implementation Committee—an additional means by which to resolve, or even avoid, disputes.[314] Established in 2012, the Implementation Committee has the objective of being a mechanism, 'to facilitate, promote and safeguard the implementation and application of and compliance with the Convention on the Protection and Use of Transboundary Watercourses and International Lakes.'[315] Additionally, the nature of the committee is described as being, 'simple, non-confrontational, non-adversarial, transparent, supportive and cooperative.'[316] Nine members, serving in their individual capacity and nominated by states, sit on the Implementation Committee. There is a mixture of both legal and scientific/technical expertise.[317] Issues may come before the Implementation Committee through a variety of

311 Rieu-Clarke & Gooch, supra note 179, at 211.

312 Art. 22(1), UNECE Water Convention.

313 Art. 22(2), UNECE Water Convention. A procedure for arbitration is set out in annex IV of the UNECE Water Convention.

314 UNECE, Decision VI/! Support to Implementation and Compliance, UN Doc. ECE/MP.WAT/37/Add.2.

315 Ibid., Annex I(1).

316 Ibid., Annex I(2).

317 The members of the committee for 2015–2018 are Ms Vanya Grigoriova, Executive Director of the Executive Environment Agency of the Ministry of Environment and Water in Bulgaria; Mr Kari Kinnunen, Director of the Lapland Regional Environmental Centre; Professor Lammars, Professor of Public International Law and former advisor to the Ministry of Foreign Affairs, the Netherlands; Professor Stephen McCaffrey, Distinguished Professor of Law, McGeorge School of Law, University of the Pacific, California; Ms Anne Schulte-Wülwer-Leidig, Deputy Head of the Secretariat of the International Commission for the Protection of the Rhine; Mr Allaksandr Stankevich, Head of the Republican Centre for Radiation Control and Environmental Monitoring in Belarus; Professor Attila Tanzi, Professor of International Law, University of Bologna; Mr Ivan Zavadsky, Secretary of the International Commission for the Protection of the Danube River; and Ms Dinara Ziganshina, Deputy Director of the Scientific Information Centre of Interstate Commission for Water Cooperation in Central Asia.

means, including by submission of a party or parties or by the Committee becoming aware of possible difficulties faced by a party or parties in implementing or complying with the Convention.[318] After investigating the issue and consulting with the party or parties concerned, the Implementation Committee has a number of measures at its disposal to support implementation and compliance. The Committee may: provide advice and facilitate assistance to individual parties and groups of parties; request and assist a party or parties to develop an action plan to facilitate implementation of and compliance with the Convention; and invite a party to submit progress reports to the Committee on efforts taken to comply with the Convention.[319] The Committee may also recommend to the Meeting of the Parties to the Convention a number of additional measures, including the provision of financial and technical assistance, training and other capacity-building measures, as well as technology transfer. The Committee may issue a statement of concern; issue declarations of non-compliance; issue cautions; suspend special rights and privileges accorded to a party under the Convention; or take other non-confrontational, non-judicial and consultative measures as appropriate.[320]

Under the Mekong Agreement, dispute-settlement mechanisms are limited. Initially, responsibility to resolve any 'difference or dispute' between two or more parties to the Mekong Agreement rests with the MRC Joint Committee and the MRC Council.[321] Failing resolution via the Joint Committee and Council, the parties are obliged to resolve the dispute, 'by negotiation through diplomatic challenges within a timely manner', and where necessary or beneficial, with, 'the assistance of mediation through an entity or party mutually agreed upon.'[322] The sum legal effect of the above provision is one of a generally non-binding and circular 'stop gap' procedure whereby the MRC and state parties to the dispute must all utilize these legally 'vague and incomplete procedures on what steps should be taken to provide remedies.'[323] It is understandable, then, that dispute resolution under the existing Mekong Agreement provisions has generally proven to be quite 'convoluted and often protracted, as illustrated in the aftermath of the Yali Falls dam.'[324]

---

318 Annex I, sections V–VII, supra note 314.

319 Annex I, section XI, supra note 314.

320 Annex I, section XI, supra note 314.

321 Art. 34, Mekong Agreement.

322 Art. 35, Making Agreement.

323 Bearden, supra note 135, at 815.

324 Bearden et al., supra note 120, at 187.

Dispute settlement is therefore another area where the UN Watercourses Convention and the UNECE Water Convention might assist in providing additional options and detail by which states can settle their disputes peacefully. In particular, the role of third parties as envisaged in both the UN Watercourses Convention and the UNECE Water Convention may prove more effective in resolving disputes. The significance of providing for specific, yet multiple, options for third-party dispute settlement is that the two global water conventions recognize that ultimately a dispute may not be able to be resolved via the cooperative efforts and good faith of the parties to the dispute alone.

A further benefit of the UN Watercourses Convention and the UNECE Water Convention is that they provide relatively detailed procedures, which clearly define the expectations within each of the sequential steps and different forums involved in resolving a dispute. In particular, the framework, standards and processes for the establishment and functioning of an independent fact-finding commission under the UN Watercourses Convention or the UNECE Water Convention Implementation Committee is fundamental to the overall dispute resolution procedures insofar as they clearly seek to demonstrate and maintain the impartiality of this forum and its recommendations. Additionally, the fact that the Annex to both conventions provides detailed standards and processes for the establishment, function and any award of an arbitral tribunal complements the above and further strengthens the overall legal framework for dispute resolution found within both Conventions. That Article 33 of the UN Watercourses Convention specifies the relevant timeframes between and within each of its relevant procedural steps is in stark contrast to the Mekong Agreement. That the Mekong Agreement refers only to 'within a timely manner' yet does not define its legal interpretation severely impacts its practical application within each of the already ambiguous process and undoubtedly leaves significant scope for varying interpretations, which can thus cause confusion and ultimately exacerbate tensions within a dispute.

Finally, the lack of any legal remedy for private citizens to seek recourse and pursue liability for harm originating in another watercourse state is also notably absent from the Mekong Agreement. Certainly, the principle of non-discrimination encapsulated in Article 32 of the UN Watercourses Convention is a notable inclusion as all of the other provisions within both instruments relate to disputes between states.[325]

325 For further analysis of the principle of non-discrimination as it applies under the UN Watercourses Convention, such as in the context of transboundary river pollution, see generally: R. Kinna, 'Non-discrimination and Liability for Transboundary Acid Mine

C Can the UN Watercourses Convention and the UNECE Water Convention Assist in Strengthening Governance in the Mekong and Beyond?

I *Becoming a Party to the UN Watercourses Convention and the UNECE Water Convention Would Be the Most Politically Feasible Option*

Widespread support for global conventions can often be stifled by a general reluctance on the part of states to cede any national sovereignty to the international realm. Nevertheless, as Hirsch maintains, '[a]ny legal framework developed to govern issues of sovereignty, redress, environmental regulation, financing arrangements and a host of other questions associated with large dams needs to go well beyond the limited arena of national law.'[326]

A common misconception of the global water conventions is that they impinge upon the national sovereignty of riparian states by restricting their ability to govern uses of international watercourses falling within their domestic jurisdictions. Rather, the function of the global water conventions is to go beyond but not usurp national sovereignty by facilitating cooperation in a manner that produces greater benefits than unilateral action can offer, and by addressing gaps in the effective governance of international watercourses.[327] Whilst the conventions address basic substantive and procedural matters, they leave much of the detail to watercourse states themselves to negotiate and agree upon.[328] Salman goes on to ably summarise the legal mandate provided under the UN Watercourses Convention to those basin states which become parties to it, whereby:

> The provisions of the Convention on those basic matters reflect a compromising language that takes into account the interests and concerns of all riparian states. The Convention calls for cooperation on the basis of sovereign equality, territorial integrity, and mutual benefit in order to attain optimal utilization of the international watercourse for the present and future generations, thus laying the general framework for mutually beneficial utilization by all the riparians.[329]

Drainage Pollution of South Africa's Rivers: Could the UN Watercourses Convention Open Pandora's Mine?' 41(3) Water International (2016) 371–391.

326 Hirsch, supra note 137, at 414.

327 UNECE, Policy Guidance Note on the Benefits of Transboundary Water Cooperation—Identification, Assessment and Communication, 2015, UN Doc. ECE/MP.Wat/47.

328 Salman, supra note 29, at 14.

329 Salman, supra note 29, at 14.

Hence, the global water conventions adopt a framework approach and possess unique legal capacity to address gaps and, in turn, improve the overall governance of international watercourses. Moreover, it is clear from the above points that not only would the global water conventions protect as well as strengthen the existing rights and duties of the MRC member states, but as regards national sovereignty, ratification would not represent an additional burden on MRC states. Rather, it would assist in the interpretation and implementation of commitments that they have already entered into as a matter of either customary international law or treaty law, including the Mekong Agreement.[330]

The MRC has up to now maintained its status as a well-funded institution, albeit one which relies upon donor governments for its funding. Yet, almost since its inception, donors have called for greater transparency within the processes and decision-making of the MRC, especially in relation to its actions under the prior notification and informed consent obligations under the Mekong Agreement.[331] Indeed, the MRC review of the PNPCA and their Guidelines was in response to donors seeking clarification of the processes and timeframes that were disputed elements between member states stemming from the Xayaburi Dam project in Laos.[332] Subsequently, this same donor query has been raised in relation to the only other mainstream dam to fall under the PNPCA process—namely the Don Sahong Dam, which is under construction in Lao.[333] These challenges faced by the MRC offer a window of opportunity to reconsider the value of states joining the two global water conventions, as a means of strengthening the implementation of the Mekong Agreement.

Previous legal analyses that compared the Mekong Agreement and its accompanying procedures against contemporary developments in the law relating to international watercourses, including the UN Watercourses Convention and the UNECE Water Convention, have overwhelmingly recommended

330 Radosevich and Olson, supra note 3; S. Pech, *UN Watercourses Convention and the Greater Mekong Sub-region*, July 2011, http://www.unwatercoursesconvention.org/images/2012/10/Mekong-and-UNWC.pdf (accessed 28 November 2016), at 51.

331 See for example, MRC, Joint Development Partner Statement, 24 June 2015, http://www.mrcmekong.org/news-and-events/speeches/joint-development-partner-statement-24-june-2015 (accessed 9 December 2016); Van Duyen, supra note 117, at 370.

332 Ibid.; A. Rieu-Clarke, 'Notification and Consultation on Planned Measures Concerning International Watercourses: Lessons from the *Pulp Mills* and *Kishenganga* Cases', 24(1) Yearbook of International Environmental Law (2014) 102–130, at 103.

333 S. Turton, 'Mekong Body Risks Losing Funds: Donors', 25 June 2015, The Phnom Penh Post.

that the Agreement be strengthened.[334] However, the majority of these studies were conducted when the UN Watercourses Convention did not look like it would enter into force, and the global relevance of the UNECE Water Convention was not fully appreciated. Moreover, at the time, no Mekong states had taken any concrete steps to become a party to either Convention, and indeed, one state (China) had voted against the UN Watercourses Convention. Rather than explore the value of the Conventions, it appeared opportune to advocate for an amendment or re-negotiation of the basin instrument in order to raise the legal standards, clarifying processes and strengthening implementation of the Mekong Agreement.[335] Bearden, for instance, maintained that:

> Although the Mekong legal regime is a viable institutional framework evidencing long-term interstate cooperation during periods of conflict, it requires amendments to achieve holistic management of water resources. With amendments, the Mekong legal regime can provide a future pathway for effective transboundary water governance of one of Southeast Asia's largest and most important international watercourses.[336]

An alternative strategy that was put forward was to advocate for a protocol to the agreement, which at the time was consider 'more politically achievable', '[g]iven the Agreement's history' and because, 'it may be difficult to change the substance of the Agreement itself.'[337]

However, revising the text or concluding an additional protocol would be extremely ambitious given the length of time and political capital required. Amending the existing provisions may not even achieve the intended outcome. Furthermore, the non-binding and somewhat convoluted nature of the key procedures and guidelines which were elaborated under the agreement, most notably the PNPCA framework, have led to some confusion between states regarding agreed-upon processes and timelines for notification and informed

334 Hirsch, supra note 137; Hirsch, et al., supra note 5; Bearden, supra note 135; Bearden, et al., supra note 18; A. Rieu-Clarke, 'Notification and Consultation Procedures Under the Mekong Agreement: Insights from the Xayaburi Controversy', 5(1) Asian Journal of International Law (2015) 143–175; Rieu-Clarke & Gooch, supra note 179; Van Duyen, supra note 117; Pech, supra note 330.

335 Bearden, supra note 135, at 815; Van Duyen, supra note 117, at 376; Pech, supra note 330.

336 Bearden, supra note 135, at 799.

337 Hirsch, et al., supra note 5, at 5. See also Bearden, supra note 135, at 815; Van Duyen, supra note 117, at 374 & 376.

consent. This confusion was demonstrated in the cases of the Xayaburi and Don Sahong projects—the first two projects that have gone through the prior consultation procedures.[338] With Lao having now submitted its third dam—Pak Beng—on the Mekong River mainstream to the MRC for prior consultation under the PNPCA and PNPCA Guidelines, the MRC claims it has learnt from the two previous prior consultation processes, yet others claim key procedural aspects of the PNPCA from those two dams still remain, to a certain extent, unclear.[339]

If the states of the Mekong were to become party to the UN Watercourses Convention and the UNECE Water Convention, it would be a more achievable means by which to ensure that customary international law was applied evenly across all of the MRC member states, as well as the basin more broadly, including China and Myanmar. Without having to sacrifice the overriding purpose and inherent 'Mekong Spirit' of the Mekong Agreement, MRC states could join the UN Watercourses Convention and the UNECE Water Convention—and as a result, not have to amend the Mekong Agreement. Finally, and most critically, joining the two global water conventions would not represent any additional burden on the MRC countries, given the advanced stage of water-related cooperation that exists within the region.[340] Rather, as noted above, it would simply be a means by which to clarify and enhance the effective implementation of previous commitments that the states have entered into pursuant to customary international law and the Mekong Agreement.

Encouraging states of the Mekong region to join the UN Watercourses Convention and the UNECE Water Convention could build upon a growing interest and support for these two global water conventions within the region. Vietnam's accession to the UN Watercourses Convention might be seen in light of a broader effort to raise awareness and promote the benefits of both

---

338 See Rieu-Clarke, supra note 334; I.C. Campbell, 'Integrated Management in the Mekong River Basin, 16(4) Ecohydrology & Hydrobiology (2016) 252–262; P. Hirsch, 'The Shifting Regional Geopolitics of Mekong Dams', 51 Political Geography (2016) 63–74; O. Hensengerth, 'Where is the Power? Transnational Networks, Authority and the Dispute over the Xayaburi Dam on the Lower Mekong Mainstream', 40 Water International (2015) 911–928.

339 MRC, 'Lao PDR Is to Undertake MRC's Prior Consultation on Its New Hydropower Development plan in Pak Beng' 7 November 2016, http://www.mrcmekong.org/news-and-events/news/mrc-statement-on-the-occasion-of-pdies-15th-anniversary-2 (accessed 5 December 2016); M. Harris 'Laos Dam Projects Put Entire Region at Risk' Bangkok Post, 17 November 2016, http://www.bangkokpost.com/opinion/opinion/1137161/laos-dam-projects-put-entire-region-at-risk (accessed 5 December 2016).

340 Radosevich & Olson, supra note 3; Pech, supra note 334, at 51.

global water conventions within the Mekong Region. Previous awareness-raising and technical capacity-building workshops on the role and relevance of the UN Watercourses Convention were conducted in 2012 by the WWF, Green Cross, the University of Dundee and Hatfield Consultants, first in Cambodia (at the national and regional levels), then in Vietnam.[341] Individually and collectively, participants were unanimous in stating that the awareness of the UN Watercourses Convention must be improved for there to be any possibility for ratification by the MRC member states.[342] Participants also called for further awareness-raising forums and in-depth technical support, together with the broad dissemination of relevant studies, and a cost-benefit analysis for states that become party to the UN Watercourses Convention.[343]

These workshops have since been built upon by those conducted in 2015 with the governments of Lao, Thailand and Cambodia. In addition, the International Union for the Conservation of Nature (IUCN) and the NGO Forum on Cambodia conducted a workshop on the two global water conventions for the Cambodian National Mekong Committee, government officials and lawyers, as well as a one-day briefing for members of the Third Commission of the National Assembly, in Phnom Penh, September 2015. This led to a co-organised WWF, IUCN, Oxfam, Conservation International and Deutsche Gesellschaft für Internationale Zusammenarbeit (GIZ) workshop in Phnom Penh in December 2015 focusing specifically on the relevance of the two global water conventions to Cambodia and its steps to accession. Several key studies have also been produced in order to investigate the role, relevance and application of the UN Watercourses Convention within the lower Mekong Basin: in 2012 by Hatfield Consultants examining the 'Relevance of the UNWC in the Greater Mekong Sub-region'; and in March 2016 a comparative legal analysis conducted by Transboundary Water Law (TWL) Global Consulting for IUCN entitled, 'A Window of Opportunity for the Mekong Basin: The UN Watercourses Convention as a Basis for Cooperation (A Legal analysis of How the UN Watercourses Convention Complements the Mekong Agreement).'[344]

341 See UN Watercourses Convention Online User's Guide, 'South and East Asia.' http://www.unwatercoursesconvention.org/global-relevance/south-and-east-asia (accessed 28 November 2016).

342 WWF UNWC Summary Regional Workshop, 2012, http://www.unwatercoursesconvention.org/global-relevance/south-and-east-asia (accessed 28 November 2016).

343 WWF UNWC Summary Regional Workshop, 2012, http://www.unwatercoursesconvention.org/global-relevance/south-and-east-asia (accessed 28 November 2016), at 17.

344 Pech, supra note 330; IUCN. 'A Window of Opportunity for the Mekong Basin: The UN Watercourses Convention as a Basis for Cooperation (A Legal analysis of How the UN Watercourses Convention Complements the Mekong Agreement)' 2016, https://www

With the 20th anniversary of the Mekong Agreement, these events and studies have been accompanied by NGOs and expert commentators calling for states to examine the added benefit of the UN Watercourses Convention to water governance in the Mekong River Basin, particularly regarding evaluation, consultation and negotiation processes for hydropower dams.[345]

Mekong states have also made an active contribution to the work of the UNECE Water Convention. For example, the MRC has contributed to the UNECE's Policy Guidance Note on the Benefits of Transboundary Water Cooperation,[346] and the work on Water and Climate Change Adaptation in Transboundary Basins.[347] Representatives from the Mekong states have also attended key meetings of the UNECE Water Convention, including the last meeting of the parties in Budapest, Hungary, November 2015.[348]

While more needs to be done to consider the benefits of the two conventions within the Mekong Region, as well as to raise awareness and secure the

---

.iucn.org/sites/dev/files/import/downloads/iucn_bridge_unwc_mra_comparison.pdf (accessed on 17 August 2016).

345 R. Kinna, 'UN Watercourses Convention: Can It Revitalise the Mekong Agreement 20 Years On?' Mekong Commons (2015, November 24) http://www.mekongcommons.org/un-watercourses-convention-can-it-revitalise-mekong-agreement-20-years-on/ (accessed on 17 August 2016); R. Kinna, 'An Alternate Past/Future for Mekong River Dams under the UN Watercourses Convention (Parts 1, 2 and 3)' Global Water Forum. (2016, April 20) http://www.globalwaterforum.org/2016/04/04/an-alternate-pastfuture-for-mekong-river-dams-under-the-un-watercourses-convention-part-1/ (accessed on 17 August 2016); J. Brunner, 'Why the Region Needs the UN Watercourses Convention' IUCN (2015, June 24). https://www.iucn.org/news_homepage/news_by_date/?21567/Why-the-region-needs-the-UNWatercourses-Convention (accessed on 17 August 2016); M. Goichot, 'UN Convention Could Help Solve Mekong Pact's Weaknesses' Phnom Penh Post (2016, January 14) http://www.phnompenhpost.com/analysis-and-op-ed/un-conventioncould-help-solve-mekong-pacts-weaknesses (accessed on 10 August 2016); R. Kinna, R., Glemet & J., Brunner, 'Reinvigorating the Mekong Spirit' Myanmar Times (2015, September 29) http://www.mmtimes.com/index.php/opinion/16719-reinvigorating-the-mekong-spirit.html (accessed on 17 August 2016); P. Suy, 'Group Proposes Signing UN Water Pact' Khmer Times (2015) http://www.khmertimeskh.com/news/16099/group-proposes-signing-un-water-pact/ (accessed on 10 August 2016).

346 UNECE, Policy Guidance Note on the Benefits of Transboundary Water Cooperation—Identification, Assessment and Communication, 2015, UN Doc. ECE/MP.Wat/47.

347 UNECE & International Network of Basin Organisations, Water and Climate Change Adaptation in Transboundary Basins: Lessons Learned and Good Practices, 2015, UN Doc. ECE/MP.WAT/45.

348 Participants in the meeting of the parties included delegates from China, Myanmar, Thailand, Vietnam and the Mekong River Commission Secretariat.

commitment of the states, such an effort would be able to build on the aforementioned positive momentum that strongly recognises the value that the two conventions can provide in supporting the implementation of the Mekong Agreement and ensuring that the basin is governed in an equitable and reasonable manner.

II *UN Watercourses Convention and the UNECE Water Convention Support the Implementation and Interpretation of the Mekong Agreement, Not Replace It*

The above comparative analysis of the three legal instruments highlights a number of areas where the UN Watercourses Convention and the UNECE Water Convention would help reinforce, rather than replace or run contrary to, the intention set out in the Mekong Agreement as well as its accompanying procedures and guidelines.

In the use of definitions, the UN Watercourses Convention and the UNECE Water Convention include reference to groundwater, which is not expressly referenced within the Mekong Agreement. Given the growing recognition of the importance of groundwater within the Mekong Region, drawing upon the UN Watercourses Convention, and the UNECE Water Convention in particular, would help strengthen this aspect of the Mekong Agreement.

Substantive provisions are more detailed in the UN Watercourses Convention compared to the Mekong Agreement, particularly in relation to the relevant factors that must be taken into account when determining what is equitable and reasonable. Similarly, compared to both the UN Watercourses Convention and the Mekong Agreement, the UNECE Water Convention provides a more detailed list of the appropriate measures that should be adopted when seeking to prevent significant harm within a transboundary context. The way in which the relationship between equitable and reasonable utilisation and no significant harm is expressed in the two global water conventions, and the UN Watercourses Convention in particular, also helps to add clarity to the relationship between the substantive norms presented in the Mekong Agreement. Both global water conventions put particular interpretative emphasis on uses of an international watercourse for the protection of vital human needs and ecosystems, which, in turn, can help support a contemporary interpretation and implementation of the more general requirements found under the Mekong Agreement.

Procedural rules that are found in the UN Watercourses Convention and the UNECE Water Convention can also help to supplement the more general requirements found in the Mekong Agreement. While much of the detail related to notification and consultation, and the more regular exchange of data and information, can be found in the procedures and guidelines adopted by the MRC, there is a question over the legal status of the latter instruments. If the lower Mekong states became parties to the UN Watercourses Convention and the UNECE Water Convention, they would enhance the legal status of the requirements of notification and prior consultation, and the regular exchange of data and information, as found in the procedures and guidelines. This would demonstrate their commitment to such procedures and add certainty to the requirements imposed upon states to notify and consult on planned measures. Additionally, becoming parties to both instruments would provide greater clarity over the requirements to notify and consult on planned measures that take place within the tributaries of the Mekong. Joining the two global water conventions would therefore expand the legal scope and application of key obligations of the Mekong Agreement insofar as the distinction between the Mekong mainstream and its tributaries, which is currently hindering the MRC in adopting a truly basin-wide approach. The UN Watercourses Convention and the UNECE Water Convention would also add additional clarity and detail as to the type of data and information that should be exchanged on a regular basis. Such detail is further expanded upon in the UNECE Water Convention, through the requirement to jointly monitor and assess the conditions of transboundary waters and to make information available to the public. Both the UN Watercourses Convention and the UNECE Water Convention would also add further detail in terms of the procedural requirements placed upon states during emergency situations. Such provisions will become increasingly relevant given the impacts of climate change within the basis and the likelihood of more extreme weather events, such as typhoons, within the basin.[349]

The UNECE Water Convention's provisions related to joint bodies could strengthen the mandate of the MRC by setting out, in a legally binding text, the key tasks of a joint body. Such tasks align well with the procedural requirements of the two global water conventions in terms of providing a forum for the exchange of information, including on planned measures, and playing a role in the EIA process.

Finally, the UN Watercourses Convention and the UNECE Water Convention could reinforce the implementation of the Mekong Agreement through their dispute-settlement mechanisms. The UN Watercourses Convention, through its stepwise and time-dependent dispute-settlement mechanisms, would strengthen the more general requirements found in the Mekong Agreement. Similarly, the UNECE Water Convention and the newly established

349 MRC, Strategic Plan 2016–2020, http://www.mrcmekong.org/assets/Publications/strategies-workprog/MRC-Stratigic-Plan-2016-2020.pdf (accessed 9 December 2016).

Implementation Committee could act as a valuable and impartial forum by which states can address any issues related to the implementation of, and compliance with, the Mekong Agreement.

The overriding purpose of ratification by states would be to create a hybrid legal architecture combining both 'hard' and 'soft' law[350] for effective governance of the Mekong River basin that goes beyond the usual dichotomy of relying primarily upon one or the other.[351] In this context, 'hard' refers to binding legal frameworks set out in the UN Watercourses Convention and the UNECE Water Convention, with their globally recognized norms as well as their binding obligations and detailed procedures; these would interlock and reinforce the relatively 'soft' and less-defined rights and obligations contained in the Mekong Agreement, along with its accompanying procedures and guidelines, which are context specific and cater to the needs and unique collective regional geo-political history of the lower Mekong Basin states.

III *Joining the UN Watercourses and the UNECE Water Convention Would Strengthen the Relationship between the Mekong Agreement and Customary International Law*

By acceding to the UN Watercourses Convention and the UNECE Water Convention, parties to the MRC would in effect align, not amend, the Mekong Agreement and its related procedures and guidelines with customary international law. As noted above, the UN Watercourses Convention is the product of a long drafting and negotiation process, which was aimed at surveying state practices and deriving key rules and principles relating to international watercourses therefrom. The UN Watercourses Convention can therefore be said to be founded upon what was already considered customary international law.[352] Similarly, while going through a different evolutionary process, the key rules and principles of the UNECE Water Convention might also be considered to be reflective of customary international law.[353] Therefore, a comparative analysis of the UN Watercourses Convention, the UNECE Water Convention and the

350 R.R. Baxter, 'International Law in "Her Infinite Variety"', 29 International and Comparative Law Quarterly (1980) 549–566.

351 Johns et al., 'Law and the Mekong River Basin: A Socio-Legal Research Agenda on the Role of Hard and Soft Law in Regulating Transboundary Water Resources', 11(1) Melbourne Journal of International Law (2010) 154–174.

352 S.M.A. Salman, 'The Helsinki Rules, The UN Watercourses Convention and the Berlin Rules: Perspectives on International Water Law', 23 International Journal of Water Resources Development (2007) 625–640.

353 A. Tanzi, O. McIntyre & A. Kolliopoulos, 'The Contribution of the UNECE Water Convention to International Water Law', in A. Tanzi et al., (eds), *The UNECE Convention*

Mekong Agreement demonstrates that there is much to be gained from the Mekong states implementing these instruments via a 'package approach.' In this regard, a 'package approach' refers to them collectively comprising a suite of internationally accepted legal norms and procedures, as accepted under customary international law, for transboundary river governance. Hence, 'the similarities between both instruments on key issues such as the focus on international or transboundary waters, or the package of substantive norms, [...] provides a strong justification for ensuring that the conventions are promoted and implemented jointly—as a"package."'[354]

In one respect, this close relationship between customary international law and the two global water conventions might be seen as a reason for *not* becoming party to either instrument. Why, for instance, would a state go through the process of treaty accession, acceptance, approval or ratification if—via customary international law—they are bound by the rights and obligations contained within that treaty anyway?[355] A counterargument would be that becoming party to a convention adds clarity to inter-state relations in two respects.

Firstly, it could be argued that even where a rule or principle is widely accepted as being reflective of customary international law, the precise contours of that rule or principle might not be widely understood or endorsed.[356] An example might be seen in the case of the duty to notify and consult over planned measures. While states might generally accept that they are under a due diligence obligation to notify other states of planned measures that may have a transboundary impact, the precise detail of that notification requirement may not be clear or may be interpreted differently by states. Even where states are not party to the UN Watercourses Convention, they would no doubt use that instrument as a guide in determining their commitments under customary international law pertaining to notification and consultation. However, greater clarity would be gained if the states were party to the UN Watercourses Convention, as it would leave less discretion for states to decide which parts

---

on the Protection and Use of Transboundary Watercourses and International Lakes—Its Contribution to International Water Cooperation (Leiden: Brill 2015) 533–539.

354 A. Rieu-Clarke and R. Kinna, 'Can Two Global UN Water Conventions Effectively Co-exist? Making the Case for a "Package Approach" to Support Institutional Coordination', 23(1) Review of European Community & International Environmental Law (2014) 15–31.

355 Such thinking might be one of the reasons slowing down states joining the UN Watercourses Convention, see Rieu-Clarke & Loures, supra note 30.

356 H. Lauterpacht, 'Codification and Development of International Law', 49(1) American Journal of International Law (1955) 16–43.

of a particular rule or principle might be reflective of customary international law or not. A similar argument might be made for the due diligence obligation to prevent significant harm. While states might accept that they have a due diligence obligation to prevent significant harm as a matter of customary international law, state perceptions on the 'appropriate measures' that they should put in place to satisfy such a due diligence requirement may differ markedly. The UNECE Water Convention offers greater clarity and certainty in this regard by setting out what the central 'appropriate measures' should be.

Secondly, it is important to bear in mind that the task of the ILC in developing the text of the UN Watercourses Convention was to codify and *progressively develop* law relating to international watercourses. While the UN Watercourses Convention might therefore be seen as generally reflective of customary international law, some rules and principles contained therein might rather be seen as reflective of existing customary international law (*lex lata*) rather than a progressive development (*lex ferenda*). The ILC does not explicitly state which provisions it considers as reflective of existing customary international law, and which it would consider as a progressive development. It is therefore up to states and other commentators to interpret which parts of a convention are reflective of customary international law and which are not. The UNECE Water Convention would also face the same challenges whereby some provisions may be reflective of customary international law, and others not. States of the Mekong Basin might therefore gain greater clarity and certainty as to what rules and principles of law apply to their relations over international watercourse by joining both conventions.

In addition, the act of joining both conventions may contribute to the strengthening of customary international law relating to international watercourses.[357] The ICJ, for example, has maintained that 'a very widespread and representative participation in ... [a] convention might suffice of itself, provided it included that of states whose interests were specially affected', to create an obligation under customary international law that is biding upon *all* states, irrespective of whether they are party to convention in question or not.[358] The Lower Mekong Basin states becoming parties to the two global water conventions could therefore play their part in helping to strengthen customary international law in relation to international watercourses. If other states were to follow their lead, and a widespread and representative body of states sharing watercourses across the world became parties to the two water conventions,

---

357 H. Thirlway, *The Sources of International Law* (Oxford: Oxford University Press 2014).

358 ICJ, North Sea Continental Shelf Cases (Federal Republic of Germany/ Denmark; Federal Republic of Germany/ Netherlands), Judgement, 20 February 1969, at 43.

then the rules and principles contained in the conventions may become binding upon all states of the Mekong Basin, including China and Myanmar.[359] Whilst such a proposition, at first glance, might be considered a big leap given that China voted against the UN Watercourses Convention in 1997, a more nuanced analysis of China's view on the convention offers encouragement. Firstly, China has entered into bilateral treaty arrangements with its neighbours that largely reflects the key rules and principles contained in both the UN Watercourses Convention and the UNECE Water Convention.[360] Secondly, the reasons for China voting against the UN Watercourses Convention might be seen as reflective of state practice and *opinio juris* at the time of adoption of the Convention, and not current thinking. For example, Burundi voted against the UN Watercourses Convention in 1997, but its subsequent state practice, including signing the Nile Cooperative Framework Agreement and becoming party to the Convention on the Sustainable Management of Lake Tanganyika, would suggest that they are now willing to accept treaty commitments that go beyond what is contained in the two global framework conventions.[361] Evidence that state opinion on the UN Watercourses Convention has evolved can also be seen in the cases of Belgium, France, Spain and Uzbekistan; while these states abstained during the recorded vote that was taken in 1997 upon adoption of the UN Watercourses Convention, they have all subsequently become parties to the Convention.[362]

359 A. D'Amato, *The Concept of Custom in International Law* (New York: Cornell University Press 1971), see also, A. D. Amato, 'The Concept of Special Custom in International Law', 63 American Journal of International Law (1969) 211–223.

360 C. Huiping, A.Rieu-Clarke & P. Wouters, 'Exploring China's Transboundary Water Treaty Practice Through the Prism of the UN Watercourses Convention', 38 Water International (2013) 217–230; P. Wouters & C. Huiping, 'China's "Soft-path" to Transboundary Water Cooperation Examined in Light of Two UN Global Water Conventions: Exploring the "Chinese Way"', 22 Journal of Water Law (2011) 229–247; P. Wouters, 'Enhancing China's Transboundary Water Cooperation—What Role for the UNECE Water Convention?', in A. Tanzi, *et al.*. (eds), *The UNECE Convention on the Protection and Use of Transboundary Watercourses and International Lakes: Its Contribution to International Water Cooperation* (London: Brill 2015) 451–565.

361 Convention on the Sustainable Management of Lake Tanganyika (2003); Agreement on the Nile River Basin Cooperative Framework (2011).

362 See recorded votes on adoption of the UN Watercourses Convention, supra note 27; and for a list of Parties to the Convention, see United Nations Office of Legal Affairs, Multilateral Treaties Deposited with the Secretary-General, https://treaties.un.org/Pages/ViewDetails.aspx?src=TREATY&mtdsg_no=XXVII-12&chapter=27&clang=_en (accessed 16 December 2016).

As it currently stands, the MRC is significantly weakened in its ability to effectively govern the Mekong River by the absence of China and Myanmar, which are not member states despite being invited to join.[363] Although China's, and to a lesser extent Myanmar's, perpetual self-exclusion from membership of the MRC via the Mekong Agreement appears to be logical given their respective locations in the upstream Mekong basin, it severely limits the MRC's mandate to adopt a truly basin-wide approach to the effective equitable and reasonable utilisation of the entire flow of the Mekong River.[364] Indeed, on this point it is worth noting that, '[a]pproximately 21 per cent of the length of the Mekong river mainstream is within Chinese territory, with this area contributing 16 per cent of the overall discharge of the river.'[365] Recent positive steps towards greater cooperation with China include the First Lancang-Mekong Cooperation Leaders' Meeting, which brought together the six countries of the Mekong.[366] Commentators have also pointed to Chinese willingness to release water from its upstream reservoirs in April 2016 to relieve the water shortages of downstream countries, as a sign of positive cooperation amongst upstream and downstream states.[367] However, others have claimed that the upstream storage is at the root cause of downstream water shortages and that such releases are actually part of normal seasonal plans, rather than altruistic acts of hydro-diplomacy by China.[368] While significant challenges in reconciling competing upstream and downstream interests over the Mekong might remain, the significance of the growing momentum in support of the two global water conventions should not be underestimated.[369] Increased

363 Bearden, supra note 135, at 811; Van Duyen, supra note 117, at 365.

364 Bearden, supra note 135, at 811; Van Duyen, supra note 117, at 365.

365 Van Duyen, supra note 117, at 365.

366 MRC, 'Lancang-Mekong Cooperation: MRC welcomes the New Initiative for Regional Cooperation by Six Countries in the Mekong Region', 31 March 2016, http://www.mrcmekong.org/news-and-events/news/lancang-mekong-cooperation-mrc-welcomes-the-new-initiative-for-regional-cooperation-by-six-countries-in-the-mekong-river-basin (accessed 28 November 2016).

367 M. Zhou, 'China and the Mekong Delta: Water Savior or Water Tyrant', 23 March 2016, The Diplomat, http://thediplomat.com/2016/03/china-and-the-mekong-delta-water-savior-or-water-tyrant (accessed 28 November 2016).

368 Ibid.

369 It could be argued that entry into force of the UN Watercourses Convention has already heightened the instrument's influence on negotiations between states over international watercourses, see for example, Z. Yihdego and A. Rieu-Clarke, 'An Exploration of Fairness in International Law Through the Blue Nile and GERD', 41 Water International (2016) 528–529.

formal endorsement of these two conventions by a wider constituency of states will no doubt enhance their value as a platform by which to negotiate cooperative arrangements between state parties and non-state parties; a platform that is premised on the need to ensure that international watercourses are governed in an equitable and sustainable manner.

IV *Additional Benefits for Mekong States in Joining the Two Global Water Conventions*

As an adjunct objective of joining the two global water conventions, there should also be a parallel focus on strengthening applicable domestic laws to align with the provisions of the UN Watercourses Convention and the UNECE Water Convention. Irrespective of how long national accession processes may take, the lower Mekong Basin states could begin actions to strengthen their domestic legislation with the aim of facilitating changes in national legislation that align with the principles and provisions of the two global water conventions. Moreover, joining the conventions could provide the necessary impetus and vehicle for each of the MRC member countries that have not already done so 'to enact specific legislation to adopt the Mekong Agreement, and to spell out the ways in which the Agreement would be consistently adopted in the particular jurisdiction.'[370] This potentially pivotal role of the two water conventions in providing a basis for parties to the Mekong Agreement seeking to update and align existing domestic water-related laws is best summed up by Pech in contending that:

> While environmental problems may be evident, a Government or Parliament may be reluctant to develop the necessary laws and institutions to address the problems [...] The state might not want to put domestic businesses at a competitive disadvantage. In this context, the multilateral agreement can elevate the international importance of a particular environmental problem, providing additional political motivation domestically (as well as internationally) to address the problem. The specific provisions of the 1997 UNWC can provide a common, basic framework for the state to follow in developing measures to address the problem. Such a common framework could help to ameliorate concerns of competitive disadvantage, and thereby facilitate domestic legislative development.[371]

370 Hirsch, et al., supra note 5, at 13.

371 Pech, supra note 330, at 72–73; See also R.A.R. Oliver, P. Moore & K. Lazarus, *Mekong Region Water Resources Decision-making: National Policy and Legal Frameworks vis-à-vis World Commission on Dams Strategic Priorities* (Bangkok: IUCN 2016).

Additionally, through the domestic process towards accession, acceptance, approval or ratification governmental departments will be required to collaborate across sectors to consider the implications of the UN Watercourses Convention on, for example, foreign investment law, environmental protection or human rights. Such collaboration may have benefits in fostering a better understanding of how to integrate legal issues pertaining to transboundary water into traditional sectors.[372]

There is also a need to analyse and identify the potential economic benefits to be achieved by MRC member states joining and implementing the two global water conventions. There are potential economic incentives to clarifying pathways, standards and expectations for cooperation, specifically in relation to the procedures for prior notification and consultation regarding planned measures such as hydropower projects with possible transboundary impacts. One instance where this benefit may have directly applied is in relation to the PNCPA process under the Mekong Agreement as applied to the Xayaburi Dam development in Laos. Both the MRC itself and the individual member states involved in this process could have benefited from having clearly defined and legally binding methods and timeframes. In relation to the PNCPA process under the Mekong Agreement as applied to the Xayaburi Dam, there were distinct 'political costs that a lack of clarity brings for all states concerned.'[373] Fragmented approaches to data and information-gathering may lead to additional costs for all interested parties, as each party seeks to unilaterally ascertain the potential risks and benefits associated with the project. Additionally, while Lao's decision to re-design the project to partially satisfy the concerns of the other lower Mekong states might be seen as a positive outcome of the Xayaburi PNPCA process, it could be argued that incorporating such concerns and changes into an early stage of the planning process would have been less costly.[374]

As the pace of dam construction rapidly accelerates and as the region's economies develop, it has become clear that the legal obligations of the Mekong Agreement and PNPCA need significant clarifying and strengthening to evolve and cope with these trends. An important turning point seems to be that the MRC and its member states finally appear to recognise this as a crucial priority. A workshop entitled 'Dialogue of Lessons Learnt from the Implementation of the PNPCA and Guidelines' was convened in February 2016

372 A. Rieu-Clarke, 'Transboundary Hydropower Projects Seen Through the Lens of Three International Legal Regimes—Foreign Investment, Environmental Protection and Human Rights', 3(1) International Journal of Water Governance (2015) 1–24.

373 Rieu-Clarke, supra note 334, at 29.

374 Rieu-Clarke, supra note 334, at 29.

by the MRC. Its stated aim was to draw lessons from states' PNPCA experiences of both the Xayaburi and Don Sahong dams in order to improve the procedures and guidelines.[375] One workshop thematic session (facilitated by one of the authors of this monograph) specifically investigated how guidance from the global water conventions and applicable international case law might support implementing legal 'best practice' standards for notification and prior consultation procedures within the PNPCA and Guidelines.[376] One of the major recommendations to emerge from this workshop was for the MRC to develop a commentary on international best practice in transboundary water governance agreements related to the PNCPA under the Mekong Agreement. In any interpretation of such a commentary, both global water conventions would form the basis and primary benchmarks for subsequent recommendations in relation to globally accepted standards for legal principles and processes for governing international rivers and how these relate to strengthening the PNPCA.

An additional benefit of membership of the UNECE Water Convention relates to the institutional framework that supports its implementation. Through the Meeting of the Parties, secretariat and various working groups, Mekong Basin states have opportunities to share their experiences with other basins across the world, which will differ in contexts but often face similar challenges. A major impetus for the work carried out under the UNECE Water Convention is the tri-annual work programme that is agreed upon by the Member States at each Meeting of the Parties. The Work Programme for 2016–2018 includes six programme areas: support for implementation and application of the convention; identifying, assessing and communicating the benefits of transboundary water cooperation; the water-food-energy-ecosystems nexus in transboundary basins; adapting to climate change in transboundary basins; opening of the Convention, promotion and partnerships; and European Union Water Initiative and National Policy Dialogues.[377] While all states are able to participate in these activities, irrespective of whether or not they are a party to the UNECE Water Convention, it might be argued that being a party shows a stronger commitment, and offers more opportunities for a state to influence the future direction of the work programme.

---

375 MRC, 'MRC Discuss Lessons Learnt From its Procedure on Water Diplomacy', 25 February 2016, http://www.mrcmekong.org/news-and-events/events/mrc-discuss-lessons-learnt-from-its-procedure-on-water-diplomacy (accessed 28 November 2016).

376 Ibid.

377 See UNECE, Report of the Meetings of the Parties on its Seventh Session, 7 July 2016, UN Doc. ECE/MP.WAT/49/Add.1.

Recommendations and Conclusions

This monograph has aimed to demonstrate that the Mekong Agreement should be strengthened through alignment with the two global water conventions, much of which reflect customary international law. Through detailed comparative legal analyses of the Mekong Agreement and its accompanying procedures and guidelines against the UN Watercourses Convention and the UNECE Water Convention, the recommendation for implementing this alignment is for Mekong states to become parties to one or both conventions. Attempting to renegotiate the Mekong Agreement's existing provisions with the expectation of increased detail and rigour is unappealing because, based on the evolution of the Agreement, such an initiative would undoubtedly take a long time and require increased resources in order for the states to negotiate and agree upon a joint text. Such an exercise may ultimately fail. Alternatively, creating a supplementary protocol to the Mekong Agreement containing the UN Watercourses Convention's and/or UNECE Water Convention's provisions would not only diminish their legally binding force (as adjuncts to the Mekong Agreement, much like the non-legally binding PNPCA and its Guidelines) but could also take significant time and resources to negotiate, agree on and enter into force. Hence, it is clear that the two reform options above are resource intensive; they undermine the legally binding framework nature of both global water conventions; and do not guarantee an outcome.

With the recent momentum behind the UN Watercourses Convention, especially Vietnam's accession leading to its entry into force, as well as the UNECE Water Convention's recent opening to global accession, there is a real alternative option to the two above for possible parallel, mutually reinforcing and normative operation of the two global water conventions in the Mekong Basin. Based on the general legal compatibility and synergies between the three legal instruments across all of their main substantive and procedural provisions, there is a compelling case for all Mekong River Basin states to become a party (parties) to one or both of the two conventions. In effect, both conventions would concomitantly clarify and strengthen the provisions of the Mekong Agreement, not replace them. In-turn, the Agreement could be valued and utilised for what it is: a broad statement of purpose for sustainable development within the Mekong region. Moreover, the MRC can then be effectively utilized within its true mandate as the crucial vehicle for cooperation, which brings the Mekong states to the negotiating table after decades of conflict and mistrust, rather than being the only dispute settlement body. Finally, based on the analysis detailed earlier, becoming party to one or both of the conventions would not present any significant additional burden on the MRC member states or the other Mekong Basin states, given that they are already committed to implement the key rules and principles that are contained in both conventions.

The authors acknowledge that accession by MRC states to one or both of the two global water conventions will require further analysis of the legal interactions between the UN Watercourses Convention and the UNECE Water Convention, the Mekong Agreement, and the Mekong Basin states. Further research on the legal process could go into more detailed analysis in relation to each country in the Mekong Basin becoming party to the UN Watercourses Convention and the UNECE Water Convention, and how this would interact with national-level laws and other bi-lateral as well as multilateral laws. Moreover, scope for future legal analysis on the effectiveness of this proposed multi-layered—some would say hybrid—regional water governance legal regime could be supported by research such as that of Hirsch and Jensen, as well as Johns et al., on the intersection between law and politics, and how national interests and domestic laws can both shape and be shaped by international legal instruments in the context of the Mekong Basin.[378] Such research could thus help build awareness and, in turn, consensus amongst the Mekong Basin states towards pursuing the broader, general recommendation 'that both the MRC and the national governments of member states initiate a process of moving from softer to harder law to support water governance in the Basin.'[379]

Now, more than 22 years after the Mekong Agreement was adopted by the lower Mekong Basin states of Thailand, Laos, Cambodia and Vietnam, and following the accession to the UN Watercourses Convention by Vietnam, and the growing momentum behind the two global water conventions, there is currently an opportunity to seek a different approach for strengthening transboundary water governance in the Mekong Basin. This monograph's detailed comparative legal analysis reveals that if the two global instruments were collectively applied as a 'package' of legal norms and procedures to support existing provisions in the Mekong Agreement, many advantages could be achieved for improved transboundary water governance in the Mekong River Basin. While there is inherent flexibility contained within the two global water conventions, they would still strengthen the implementation and interpretation of the Agreement in a number of important areas, including the treatment

378 Hirsch, P. & Jensen, K.M. (2006). National Interests and Transboundary Water Governance in the Mekong. Australian Mekong Resource Centre, University of Sydney, Australia; Johns, F., Saul, B., Hirsch, P., Stephens, T. & Boer, B. (2010). Law and the Mekong River Basin: A Social-Legal Research Agenda on the Role of Hard and Soft Law in Regulating Transboundary Water Resources Melbourne Journal of International Law 11(1), 154.

379 Ibid., at xvii.

of groundwater, the 'package' of substantive norms, the level of detail pertaining to legally binding procedural rules, and the step-wise and pragmatic approach to dispute settlement. Moreover, a concerted effort by the Mekong states to become parties to the global water conventions would also strengthen customary international law both generally and in the region, and provide a solid legal platform by which upstream and downstream states can negotiate more effectively than is currently the case. Ultimately, in implementing the UN Watercourses Convention and the UNECE Water Convention, in parallel with the Mekong Agreement, riparian states would have a more comprehensive and enforceable framework to meet the pressing challenges faced within the Mekong River Basin.

Bibliography

Backer, B., 'The Mekong River Commission: Does It Work, and How Does the Mekong Basin's Geography Influence Its Effectiveness?', 26(4) Journal of Current Southeast Asian Affairs (2007) 32–56.

Barnidge, R.P., 'The Due Diligence Principle Under International Law', 8(1) International Community Law Review (2006) 81–121.

Baxter, R.R., 'International Law in "Her Infinite Variety"', 29 International and Comparative Law Quarterly (1980) 549–566.

Bearden, B., Rieu-Clarke A. & Pech, S., 'Mekong Basin', in Rocha Loures F. & A. Rieu-Clarke A., (eds.), *The UN Watercourses Convention in Force—Strengthening International Law for Transboundary Water Management* (Abingdon: Routledge 2013) 180–188.

Bearden, B., 'The Legal Regime of the Mekong River: A Look Back and Some Proposals for the Way Ahead', 12 Water Policy (2010) 798–821.

Bearden, B., 'Following the Proper Channels: Tributaries in the Mekong Legal Regime', 14(6) Water Policy (2012) 991–1014.

Boer, B., Saul, B., Johns, F., Scurrah, N., & Hirsch, P., *The Mekong: A Socio-legal Approach to River Basin Development* (Abingdon: Routledge 2015).

Bogdanović, S., *International Law of Water Resources* (London: Kluwer Law International 2001).

Bonheur N. & Lane, B.D., 'Natural Resources Management for Human Security in Cambodia's Tonle Sap Biosphere Reserve', 5(1) Environmental Science & Policy (2002) 33–41.

Browder, G., 'An Analysis of the Negotiations for the 1995 Mekong Agreement', 5(2) International Negotiations (2000) 237–261.

Browder, G. & Ortolano, L., 'The Evolution of an International Water Resources Management Regime in the Mekong River Basin', 40 Natural Resources Journal 499–531.

Brunner, J. (2015, June 24). Why the region needs the UN Watercourses Convention. IUCN. Available at https://www.iucn.org/news_homepage/news_by_date/?21567/Why-the-region-needs-the-UNWatercourses-Convention.

Campbell, I.C., 'Integrated Management in the Mekong River Basin', 16(4) Ecohydrology & Hydrobiology (2016) 252–262.

Caponera, D.A., 'The Legal Aspects of Mekong River Projects', 16 Journal of Power and River Valley Development (1966) 35–38.

Chenoweth, J., 'International River Basin Management: Data and Information Exchange Under International Law and the Case of the Mekong River Basin', 18(2) Journal of Energy & Natural Resources Law (2000) 142–158.

D'Amato, A., *The Concept of Custom in International Law* (New York : Cornell University Press 1971).

D.Amato, A., 'The Concept of Special Custom in International Law', 63 American Journal of International Law (1969) 211–223.

Dugan, P.J., et al., 'Fish Migration, Dams, and Loss of Ecosystem Services in the Mekong Basin', 39(4) AMBIO (2010) 344–348.

Gao, Q., *A Procedural Framework for Transboundary Water Management in the Mekong River Basin* (London: Brill 2014).

Garschagen, M., et al., 'Socio-Economic Development in the Mekong Delta: Between the Prospects for Progress and the Realms of Reality', in Renaud, F.G. & Kuenzer, C. (eds.), *The Mekong Delta System: Interdisciplinary Analyses of a River Delta* (Dordrecht: Springer 2012).

Gleick, P.H., 'The Human Right to Water', 1 Water Policy (1998) 487–503.

Goh, E., *Developing the Mekong: Regionalism and Regional Security in China-Southeast Asian Relations* (Routledge, Abingdon 2007).

Goichot, M., 'UN Convention Could Help Solve Mekong Pact's Weaknesses' Phnom Penh Post, 14 January 2016, http://www.phnompenhpost.com/analysis-and-op-ed/un-conventioncould-help-solve-mekong-pacts-weaknesses.

Ha, K., et al., *Current Status and Issue of Groundwater in the Mekong River Basin* (Bangkok: KIGAM, CCOP & UNESCO 2015).

Halbertsma, H.G., 'Legal Aspects of the Mekong River System', 34(1) Netherlands International Law Review (1987) 25–53.

Harris, M., 'Laos Dam Projects Put Entire Region at Risk', Bangkok Post, 17 November 2016, http://www.bangkokpost.com/opinion/opinion/1137161/laos-dam-projects-put-entire-region-at-risk.

Hensengerth, O., 'Trans-boundary River Cooperation and the Regional Public Good: The Case of the Mekong River', 31 Contemporary Southeast Asia : A Journal of International Strategic Affairs (2009) 326–349.

Hensengerth, O., 'Where is the Power? Transnational Networks, Authority and the Dispute Over the Xayaburi Dam on the Lower Mekong Mainstream', 40 Water International (2015) 911–928.

Hey, E., 'The Watercourses Convention: To What Extent Does it Provide a Basis for Regulating Uses on International Watercourses', 7 Review of European, Comparative & International Environmental Law (1998) 291–300.

Hirsch, P., et al., *National Interests and Trans-boundary Water Governance in the Mekong* (Sydney: Mekong Resource Centre 2006).

Hirsch , P., 'The Shifting Regional Geopolitics of Mekong Dams', 51 Political Geography (2016) 63–74.

Hirsch, P., 'Water Governance and Catchment Management in the Mekong Region', 15(2) The Journal of Environment & Development (2006).

Hirsh, P., 'Beyond the Nation State: Natural Resource Conflict and National Interest in Mekong Hydropower Development', 29(3) Golden Gate University Law Review (1999) 399–414.

Huiping, C., Rieu-Clarke A. & Wouters, P.K., 'Exploring China's Transboundary Water Treaty Practice Through the Prism of the UN Watercourses Convention', 38 Water International (2013) 217–230.

ICEM, *MRC Strategic Environmental Assessment (SEA) of Hydropower on the Mekong Mainstream: Summary of the Final Project* (Hanoi: MRC 2010).

IUCN, 'A Window of Opportunity for the Mekong Basin: The UN Watercourses Convention as a Basis for Cooperation (A Legal Analysis of How the UN Watercourses Convention Complements the Mekong Agreement)' IUCN (2016), 27pp.

Jacobs, J.W., 'The Mekong River Commission: Transboundary Water Resources Planning and Regional Security', 168(4) The Geographical Journal (2002) 354–364.

Johns et al., 'Law and the Mekong River Basin: A Socio-Legal Research Agenda on the Role of Hard and Soft Law in Regulating Transboundary Water Resources', 11(1) Melbourne Journal of International Law (2010) 154–174.

Keskinen, M., Mehtonen, K. & Varis, O., 'Transboundary Cooperation vs. Internal Ambitions: The Role of China and Cambodia in the Mekong Region', in I. Nevelina, et al. (eds), *International Water Security: Domestic Threats and Opportunities* (Tokyo: UN University Press 2008) 79–109.

Kinna, R., 'Non-discrimination and Liability for Transboundary Acid Mine Drainage Pollution of South Africa's Rivers: Could the UN Watercourses Convention Open Pandora's Mine?' 41(3) Water International (2016) 371–391.

Kinna, R., 'UN Watercourses Convention: Can it Revitalise the Mekong Agreement 20 Years On?' Mekong Commons, 24 November 2015, http://www.mekongcommons.org/un-watercourses-convention-can-it-revitalise-mekong-agreement-20-years-on/.

Kinna, R., 'An Alternate Past/Future for Mekong River Dams under the UN Watercourses Convention (Parts 1, 2 and 3)',Global Water Forum, 20 April 2016, http://

www.globalwaterforum.org/2016/04/04/an-alternate-pastfuture-for-mekong-river-dams-under-the-un-watercourses-convention-part-1/.

Kinna, R., Glemet, R., & Brunner, J., 'Reinvigorating the Mekong Spirit', Myanmar Times, 29 September 205, http://www.mmtimes.com/index.php/opinion/16719-reinvigorating-the-mekong-spirit.html.

Kirmani, S.S., 'Water, Peace and Conflict Management: The Experience of the Indus and Mekong River Basins', 15(4) Water International (1990) 200–205.

Kite, G., *Developing a Hydrological Model for the Mekong Basin—Impacts of Basin Development on Fisheries Productivity* (Colombo: IWMI 2000).

Kulesza, J., *Due Diligence in International Law* (London: Brill 2016).

Lamberts, D., 'The Tonle Sap Lake as a Productive Ecosystem', 22(3) Water Resources Development (2006) 481–495.

Lauterpacht, H., 'Codification and Development of International Law', 49(1) American Journal of International Law (1955) 16–43.

Leb, C., *Cooperation in the Law of Transboundary Water Resources* (Cambridge: Cambridge University Press 2013).

Lee G. & Scurrah, N., *Power and Responsibility—The Mekong River Commission and Lower Mekong Mainstream Dams* (Sydney: Oxfam Australia & University of Sydney 2009).

Lee, J., *Preservation of Ecosystems of International Watercourses and the Integration of Relevant Rules—An Interpretative Mechanism to Address the Fragmentation of International Law* (London: Brill 2014).

McCaffrey, S.C., 'The Contribution of the UN Convention on the Law of the Non-navigational Uses of International Watercourses', 1(3/4) International Journal of Global Environmental Issues (2001) 250–263.

McCaffrey, S.C., 'The Evolution of the Law of International Watercourses', 5(2) Austrian Journal of Public and International Law (1996) 87–111.

McCaffrey, S.C., 'An Assessment of the Work of the International Law Commission', 36 Natural Resources Journal (1996) 297–318.

McIntyre, O., *Environmental Protection of International Watercourses under International Law* (London: Ashgate Publishing Group 2007).

McIntyre, O., 'The Emergence of an "Ecosystem Approach" to the Protection of International Watercourses under International Law', 13(1) Review of European, Comparative & International Environmental Law (2004) 2–14.

McIntyre, O., 'The Protection of Freshwater Ecosystems Revisted: Towards a Common Understanding of the "Ecosystems Approach" to the Protection of Transboundary Resources', 32(1) Review of European, Comparative & International Environmental Law (2014) 88–95.

McIntyre, O., 'The Proceduralisation and Growing Maturity of International Water Law: Case Concerning Pulp Mills on the River Uruguay (Argentina v. Uruguay)', 22(3) Journal of Environmental Law (2010) 475–497.

Middleton, J. Garcia & T. Foran, 'Old and New Hydropower Players in the Mekong Region: Agendas and Strategies', in Molle, F., Foran, T. & Käkönen, M., *Contested Waterscapes in the Mekong Region—Hydropower, Livelihoods and Governance* (London, Earthscan 2009) 23–54.

Mirumachi, N., *Transboundary Water Politics in the Developing World* (Abingdon: Routledge 2015),

Molle, F., Foran, T. & Käkönen, M., *Contested Waterscapes in the Mekong Region—Hydropower, Livelihoods and Governance* (London, Earthscan 2009)

Myint, T., 'Democracy in Global Environmental Governance: Issues, Interests, and Actors in the Mekong and the Rhine', 10(1) Indiana Journal of Global Legal Studies (2003) 287–314.

MRC, 'MRC Discuss Lessons Learnt From its Procedure on Water Diplomacy', 25 February 2016, http://www.mrcmekong.org/news-and-events/events/mrc-discuss-lessons-learnt-from-its-procedure-on-water-diplomacy.

MRC, Fish Migrations of the Lower Mekong River Basin: Implications for Development, Planning and Environmental Management', (Phnom Penh: MRC 2002).

MRC, 'Lao PDR Is to Undertake MRC's Prior Consultation on Its New Hydropower Development Plan in Pak Beng', 7 November 2016. Available from: http://www.mrcmekong.org/news-and-events/news/mrc-statement-on-the-occasion-of-pdies-15th-anniversary-2/.

MRC, *State of the Basin Report 2010* (Vientiane: MRC 2010).

Nollkaemper, A., 'The Contribution of the International Law Commission to International Water Law: Does it Reverse the Flight from Substance?', 27 Netherlands Yearbook of International Law (1996) 39–73.

Oliver, R.A.R., Moore, P. & Lazarus, K., *Mekong Region Water Resources Decision-making: National Policy and Legal Frameworks vis-à-vis World Commission on Dams Strategic Priorities* (Bangkok: IUCN 2016).

Orr, S., et al., 'Dams on the Mekong River: Lost Fish Protein and the Implications for Land and Water Resources', 22(4) Global Environmental Change (2012), 925–932.

Osborne, M., *River at Risk: The Mekong and Water Politics of China and Southeast Asia* (London: Longueville Media 2004).

Paisley, R.K., Weiler, P. & Henshaw, T., 'Trans-boundary Waters Governance Through The Prism of the Mekong River Basin', in Gray, N., Holley, C. & Rayfuse, R. (eds), *Trans-jurisdictional Water Law and Governance* (London: Routledge 2016) 43–61.

Paisley, R.K., 'Adversaries into Partners: International Water Law and the Equitable Sharing of Downstream Benefits', 3(2) Melbourne Journal of International Law (2002) 280–301.

Pittock, J, Dumaresq, D. & Bassi, A., 'Modeling the Hydropower—Food Nexus in Large River Basin: A Mekong Case Study', 8 Water (2016) 1–18.

Pech, S., *UN Watercourses Convention and the Greater Mekong Sub-region*, July 2011, http://www.unwatercoursesconvention.org/images/2012/10/Mekong-and-UNWC.pdf (accessed 28 November 2016).

Pech, S. & Sunada, K., 'Population Growth and Natural-Resources Pressures in the Mekong River Basin', 37 :3, AMBIO (2008) 219–224.

Radosevic, G.E. & Olson, D.C., 'Existing and Emerging Basin Arrangements in Asia: Mekong River Commission Case Study', paper presented at World Bank, Third Workshop on River Basin Institution Development, 24 June 1999, Washington, D.C.

Renaud, F.G. & Kuenzer, C. (eds.), *The Mekong Delta System: Interdisciplinary Analyses of a River Delta* (Dordrecht: Springer 2012).

Rieu-Clarke, A., 'Notification and Consultation on Planned Measures Concerning International Watercourses: Lessons from the *Pulp Mills* and *Kishenganga* Cases', 24(1) Yearbook of International Environmental Law (2014) 102–130.

Rieu-Clarke, A., 'Notification and Consultation Procedures Under the Mekong Agreement: Insights from the Xayaburi Controversy', 5(1) Asian Journal of International Law (2015) 143–175.

Rieu-Clarke, A., 'Determining Sovereign Rights and Duties over International Watercourses: The Contribution of the International Law Commission and the UN General Assembly', in T. Tvedt, O. McIntyre & T.K. Woldetsadik, (eds), *A History of Water—Sovereignty and International Water Law* (London: I.B. Tauris 2015) 149–174.

Rieu-Clarke, A., 'Transboundary Hydropower Projects Seen Through the Lens of Three International Legal Regimes—Foreign Investment, Environmental Protection and Human Rights', 3(1) International Journal of Water Governance (2015) 1–24.

Rieu-Clarke, A. & Kinna, R., 'Can Two Global UN Water Conventions Effectively Coexist? Making the Case for a "Package Approach" to Support Institutional Coordination', 23(1) Review of European, Comparative & International Environmental Law (2014) 15–31.

Rieu-Clarke, A. & Gooch, G., 'Governing the Tributaries of the Mekong—The Contribution of International Law and Institutions to Enhancing Equitable Cooperation over the Sesan', 22 Pacific McGeorge Global Business and Development Law Journal (2009) 193–224.

Rieu-Clarke, A. & Loures, F.R., 'Still Not in Force: Should States Support the 1997 UN Watercourses Convention?' 18(2) Review of European, Comparative & International Environmental Law (2009) 185–197.

Rieu-Clarke, A., 'Remarks on the Drafting History of the Convention' in A. Tanzi, *et al.* (eds), *The UNECE Convention on the Protection and Use of Transboundary Watercourses and International Lakes: Its Contribution to International Water Cooperation* (London: Brill 2015) 3–14.

Rieu-Clarke, A. & Spray, C., 'Ecosystems Services and International Water Law: Towards a More Effective Determination and Implementation of Equity?'16(2) Potscheftstroom Electronic Review (2013) 12–65.

Salman, S.M.A., 'The United Nations Watercourses Convention Ten Years Later: Why Has its Entry into Force Proven Difficult?', 32 *Water International* (2007) 1–15.

Salman, S.M.A., 'The Helsinki Rules, The UN Watercourses Convention and the Berlin Rules: Perspectives on International Water Law', 23 International Journal of Water Resources Development (2007) 625–640.

Salman, S.M.A., 'Entry into Force of the UN Watercourses Convention: Why Should It Matter?', 31 International Journal of Water Resources Development (2014) 4–16.

Schroeder-Wildberg, E., 'The 1997 International Watercourses Convention—Background and Negotiations', Working Paper on Management in Environmental Planning, 2002, https://www.landschaftsoekonomie.tu-berlin.de/fileadmin/a0731/uploads/publikationen/workingpapers/wp00402.pdf (accessed 24 November 2016).

Shuval, H., 'Meeting Vital Human Needs: Equitable Resolution of Conflicts over Shared Water Resources of Israelis and Palestinians', in H. Shuval & H. Dweik, *Water Resources in the Middle East* (Berlin: Springer 2007) 3–16.

Sneddon, C. and Fox, C., 'Rethinking Transboundary Waters: Critical Hydropolitics of the Mekong Basin', 25 Political Geography (2006) 181–202.

Suhardiman, D. & Giordano, M., 'Legal Plurality: An Analysis of Power Interplay in Mekong Hydropower', 104(5) Annals of the Association of American Geographers (2014) 973–988.

Suy, P., (2015). 'Group Proposes Signing UN Water Pact', Khmer Times. Available from: http://www.khmertimeskh.com/news/16099/group-proposes-signing-un-water-pact/.

Tanzi, A., Kolliopoulos A. & Nikiforova, N., 'Normative Features of the UNECE Water Convention', in A. Tanzi, *et al.* (eds), *The UNECE Convention on the Protection and Use of Transboundary Watercourses and International Lakes: Its Contribution to International Water Cooperation* (London: Brill 2015) 116–129.

Tanzi, A., et al. (eds), *The UNECE Convention on the Protection and Use of Transboundary Watercourses and International Lakes: Its Contribution to International Water Cooperation* (London: Brill 2015) 116–129.

Thirlway, H., *The Sources of International Law* (Oxford: Oxford University Press 2014).

Turton, S. 'Mekong Body Risks Losing Funds: Donors', 25 June 2015, The Phnom Penh Post.

Urban, F., et al., 'An Analysis of China's Investment in the Hydropower Sector in the Greater Mekong Sub-Region', 15(2) Environment, Development and Sustainability (2013) 301–324.

UNECE, The Economic Commission for Europe Water Convention and the United Nations Watercourses Convention—An Analysis of their Harmonized Contribution to International Water Law, 2015, UN Doc. ECE/MP.WAT.42.

Utton, A.E., 'Which Rule Should Prevail in International Water Disputes: That of Reasonableness or That of No Harm', 36 Natural Resources Journal (1996) 635–641.

Van Duyen, N., 'The Inadequacies of Environmental Protection Mechanisms in the Mekong River Basin Agreement', 6 Asia Pacific Journal of Environmental Law (2001) 349–376.

Vinogradov, S., Wouters, P.K. & Jones, P., *Transforming Potential Conflict into Cooperation Potential: The Role of International Water Law* (Paris: UNESCO 2003)

Walling, D.E., 'The Changing Sediment Load of the Mekong River', 37(3) AMBIO (2008) 150–157.

Wouters, P.K., 'An Assessment of Recent Developments in International Watercourse Law through the Prism of the Substantive Rules Governing Use Allocation', 36(2) Natural Resources Journal (1996) 417–439.

Wouters, P.K., 'Enhancing China's Transboundary Water Cooperation—What Role for the UNECE Water Convention?', in A. Tanzi, *et al.* (eds), *The UNECE Convention on the Protection and Use of Transboundary Watercourses and International Lakes: Its Contribution to International Water Cooperation* (London: Brill 2015) 451–565.

Wouters, P.K. & Huiping, C., 'China's "Soft-path" to Transboundary Water Cooperation Examined in light of Two UN Global Water Conventions: Exploring the "Chinese Way"', 22 Journal of Water Law (2011) 229–247.

Wouters, P.K., et al., *Sharing Transboundary Waters—An Integrated Assessment of Equitable Entitlement* (Paris: UNESCO 2005).

Yasuda, *Rules, Norms and NGO Advocacy Strategies: Hydropower Development in the Mekong River* (Abingdon: Routledge 2015).

Zawahri, N. & McLaughlin, S., 'Fragmented Governance in International Rivers: Negotiating Bilateral Versus Multilateral Treaties', 44 International Studies Quarterly (2011) 835–858.

www.ingramcontent.com/pod-product-compliance
Lightning Source LLC
Chambersburg PA
CBHW031332230926
51848CB00001B/195
9789004345690